MW01327310

THE CHEFS
OF
HILTON HEAD

Compiled by
John Sams Colquhoun

Southern Islands Publishing
Beaufort, South Carolina

THE CHEFS OF HILTON HEAD

Third Edition
Copyright © 2000
by Southern Islands Publishing

Original design by Robin Koppernaes
Write Ideas, Beaufort, SC

Revised and Edited
by Kelly Newnham and Jacki Martin
KC Newnham & Company
Beaufort, SC

Copies of *The Chefs of Hilton Head*
may be obtained by writing to
Southern Islands Publishing
PO Box 69
Beaufort, SC 29901

ISBN 0-9655662-3-4

Acknowledgements

The cover design is from an original watercolor by Savannah, Georgia artist Ray Ellis. For more information, please contact him at 205 W. Congress Street, Savannah, Georgia 31401; (912) 234-3537.

Minor's products, courtesy of Heidi and David Sievers, owners of All Serve, Inc. and distributors of Minor's bases, 1-800-827-8328.

Old Bay® seasonings, courtesy of McCormick Spices, Hunt Valley, Maryland, 1-800-632-5847.

Tabasco pepper sauce, courtesy of Paul McIlhenny, The McIlhenny Co., Avery Island, Louisiana.

Southern Islands Publishing would like to give special thanks to the following: Faith Nance, Birmingham, Alabama; Dottie Trivison, Food Editor of *The Island Packet*; and of course all of the chefs and restaurant owners whose recipes made this book possible!

TABLE OF CONTENTS

Introduction

This collection of recipes is from some of the finest chefs and restaurants on Hilton Head Island. For your convenience, a restaurant guide follows.

The chefs in this book not identified with a restaurant have moved on to other positions. They were, however, at one time a chef on Hilton Head and their recipes continue to be presented in this book as examples of the finest in innovative Southern cuisine.

John Colquhoun

Restaurant Guide

Alligator Grille
16 Coligny Plaza
842-4888
Serving an American mosaic of contemporary regional cuisine. Popular Chef Michael Diehl, President of Hilton Head's Chefs' Association, presides.

Anna's Beachside Cafe
110 Beach Market (at Coligny Circle off N. Forest Beach)
842-8797
Unique Mediterranean Cuisine with a flair includes seafood, duck, chicken, flank steak, lambchops and pizza.

Antonio's
Village at Wexford
842-5505
Serving authentic Southern Italian cuisine for over 15 years.

Aunt Chilada's
69 Pope Avenue
785-7700
Offering delicious Mexican, Italian, seafood and house specials.

Belfair Country Club
200 Oaks Boulevard (Highway 280, Bluffton)
842-1100
Private, members and guests only clubhouse restaurant on the banks of the Colleton River. 10 minutes from Hilton Head.

Boathouse II
397 Squire Pope Road
681-3663
Waterfront restaurant featuring Lowcountry favorites and fresh from the sea specialties.

Brian's
1301 Main Street Village
681-6001
Contemporary dining in an elegant atmosphere, serving "only the finest quality product."

Café Belfair
Sheridan Park, Hwy 278, (5 minutes from bridge)
815-7818
Casual fine dining in a friendly atmosphere. Fresh fish specials daily. Steaks, lamb shanks, chicken, veal and pasta. Full bar and fine wines.

Café Europa
At the Lighthouse in Harbour Town
671-3399
One of the most popular and picturesque restaurants, Café Europa has "the" view on Hilton Head with the most spectacular sunsets in town. A good selection of seafood, pasta, steaks and more at the lighthouse in Harbour Town. Bev, Lou and Lisa Gerber, your hosts.

Captain's Seafood
Highway 278 (1/2 mile south of Shelter Cove)
686-3200
Retail fish market and restaurant serving a wide variety of the freshest seafood. Childrens menu. Catering available. Party trays.

Cattail's
Moss Creek Village (Just over the bridge)
837-7000
Outstanding American cuisine. Proprietor/Chef Mehdi Varedi uses only the freshest ingredients to provide an innovative combination of flavors and textures.

The Captain's Table
Oceanfront at The Sea Crest
686-4300
Fresh seafood, prime beef, lamb and pastas. Very attractive restaurant.
Lunch, dinner and Sunday brunch. Highly recommended restaurant.
Reservations recommended.

Charlie's
Mid Island on Hwy 278 (next to Palmetto Dunes entrance)
785-9277
Specializing in fish entrées. Also offering veal, beef, lamb, and duck.

Corner Market Cafe
Coligny Plaza (next to Piggly Wiggly)
785-4426
Gourmet shoppe, baked goods, deli and catering. Duck salad,
rotisserie chicken, wide selection of sandwiches.

C.Q's
Under the Oaks in Harbour Town
671-2779
Serving the island's "primest rib," along with char-grilled steaks, fresh
seafood, tasty pastas and chef's specials. Patio dining available.

Crane's Tavern
26 New Orleans Road
341-2333
Excellent steakhouse featuring very attractive decor. Chicken and a
great selection of fresh seafood are offered as is a veal chop. A family
tradition of excellence in quality and value for over seventy years.

Crazy Crab Harbour Town
149 Lighthouse Road
363-CRAB (2722)
Seafood house, lowcountry recipes, chicken, steaks, live Maine lobsters and daily Chef's specials. Lunch and Dinner. Visit our other
Crazy Crab on Hwy. 278 next to Hilton Head Museum.

Harbourmaster's
Waterfront at Shelter Cove Harbour
785-3030
Outstanding "creative cuisine." Seafood, steaks, veal, chops, chicken and pastas. Specials nightly. Three levels of dining. Extensive wine list. Outdoor deck.

Hyatt Regency
    The Café
    785-1234
    Featuring the island's most complete seafood buffet.
    Hemingway's
    785-1234
    Serving an excellent selection of beef, game and seafood. Both oceanfront.

Julep's
Located in the Gallery of Shops (near Sea Pines Circle)
842-5857
Fine food and gracious hospitality with a southern flair. Excellent menu includes steak, chicken, duck, seafood and game. Sam and Melissa Cochran, your hosts.

Just Pasta Café
Coligny Plaza oceanside (facing North Forest Beach Drive)
686-3900
A wide variety of pasta with numerous sauces. Manicotti, ziti, lasagne, cannelloni, chicken parmesan, scampi, seafood Fra Diavolo and fresh fish specials daily. Also fresh baked breads and desserts.

The Kingfisher
On Shelter Cove Harbour
842-6400
Offering an excellent selection of well prepared Italian specialties and fresh, local seafood. Chef Geoff Fennessey graduated #1 in his class from the Chef's Institute of America.

Lagniappe (Lan-yap)
The Village at Wexford
341-3377
Charming restaurant and art gallery. A well-rounded menu featuring veal, fresh seafood and pasta specialties. Chicken, pork tenderloin and duck. Aaron and Sharen Glugover, Proprietors.

Market Street Cafe
Coligny Plaza (facing N. Forest Beach Drive)
686-4976
Well-prepared Greek and Mediterranean specialties including Mousaka, Pastitsio and Spanakopita. Subs, grinders, gyros, soups, salads, pizzas and baklava all offered.

Mostly Seafood
The Hilton Oceanfront Resort, Palmetto Dunes
842-8000
Causual fine dining in a newly-renovated restaurant serving "mostly seafood" in a contemporary American style. Nightly specials. Vintner dinners. Elegant presentation by Chef Michael Wallace.

Neno Il Toscano
105 Festival Center (across from Wal-Mart)
342-2400
Authentic Northern Italian cuisine. Fresh pasta, seafood and veal creations, chicken and steaks.

Old Fort Pub
65 Skull Creek Drive in Hilton Head Plantation
681-2386
Richly deserved reputation for fine Lowcountry cuisine including baked fish Daufuskie, she-crab soup and oyster pie. Overlooking Skull Creek and the Intracoastal Waterway.

Okatie Creek Restaurant
Sun City Hilton Head
705-4006
Cozy dining room with fireplace and golf course views serving chicken, beef, pork, seafood and daily chef specials. Lunch and dinner. Open to the public. Chef Roger Howard.

Primo!
Orleans Plaza
785-2343
The best in contemporary Italian cuisine for more than 12 years. Veal, pork, beef, seafood and chicken along with freshly made pastas.

Portz Restaurant
Crowne Plaza Resort at Shipyard Plantation
842-2400
Mediterranean cuisine with a Lowcountry flair. Primarily seafood. Daily specials, chicken, pork, duck and lamb available.

Reilly's North
Port Royal Plaza
681-7582
An island favorite serving steaks, seafood, pasta and nightly specials. "Kid's Menu" available. Visit Reilly's South at Sea Pines Circle. Phone 842-4414.

Rendezvous Café
At The Gallery of Shops off Sea Pines Circle
785-5070
Attractive French bistro featuring outstanding fare from the provinces of France. Good selection of seafood, veal, chicken and beef.

Scott's Fish Market
Shelter Cove Harbour
785-7575
Waterfront restaurant and bar. Excellent fresh seafood and prime beef, chicken and pasta. Indoor and outdoor dining.

The Sea Shack
6 Pope Avenue (Executive Park Road behind Hofbrauhaus)
785-2464
Huge selection of fresh seafood excellently prepared by popular island Chef Gary Williams. Burger, Chicken and steak specials available. A personal favorite!

Sigler's Rotisserie, "The Chef's Place"
Hwy 278 Sheridan Park (5 minutes from bridge)
815-5030
Chef Michael Sigler, former chef at the Westin Resort, Hilton Head, offers seafood, pork, lamb, chicken and beef. "Open Kitchen."

Spartina Grill
70 Marshland Road
689-2433
Outstanding Island fare includes "Voo Doo" Pasta, Plantation Stewpot, Rattlesnake Chicken and Lowcountry Seafood Saute. Richard and Leah Vaughan, proprietors.

Starfire
Orleans Plaza
785-3434
Unusually well-prepared classic American dishes. Menu changes weekly. Chef Keith Josefiak's servings include roasted chicken, crawfish and pasta, lamb shanks, veal, beef and more.

Stripes, An American Grill
Courtyard Building (opposite Park Plaza, near Sea Pines Circle)
686-4747
Outstanding American regional cuisine includes Filet "au poivre," osso buco, seafood, duck, and Angus Beef meatloaf with lumpy mashed potatoes. Chef Steve Hancotte was #1 in his class at CIA.

Sunset Grille
On the north end across from Windmill Harbour At Outdoor Resorts Marina
689-6744
Waterfront dining. Beautiful view. Good selection of seafood, beef, pork, chicken and pastas. Fresh baked pastries and desserts.

Taste of Thailand
807 William Hilton Parkway (behind Charlies)
341-6500
A unique dining experience of traditional Thai cuisine featuring beef, pork, chicken, duck and seafood with a wide variety of spices, sauces and preparations.

Tavern on the Creek
Skull Creek Marina in Hilton Head Plantation
689-9565
Genuinely elegant waterfront restaurant with spectacular sunsets. Seafood, beef, veal, chicken and rack of lamb among the offerings by award winning Chef Michael Ramey.

Two Eleven Park
211 Park Plaza
686-5212
Offering seafood, steaks, pasta, gourmet pizzas and nightly specials with a "Southern Fusion" twist. In addition, choose from over 200 selections of wine, 75 by the glass.

The Westin Hotel
    The Barony
    681-4000
    Quiet, intimate atmosphere with a sophisticated flair. Excellent selection of seafood, beef, veal, duck and chicken. Extensive wine list.
    The Carolina Café
    681-4000
    Casual dining. Seafood extravaganza buffet 7 nights a week.

Useful Information

SAN FRANCISCO HERB COMPANY
1-800-227-4530
www.sfherb.com

ATLANTIC SPICE COMPANY
1-800-316-7965
www.atlanticspice.com

ALL SERVE, INC.
distributor's of Minor's bases
1-800-827-8328
www.soupbase.com

McCORMICK SPICES
1-800-632-5847
www.mccormick.com

USA MEAT & POULTRY HOTLINE
1-800-535-4555
www.fsif.usda.gov

Soups

1

Acorn Squash and Crawfish Chowder

Heat the clarified butter in a large skillet. Sauté the onion, celery, carrots, pecan pieces, potatoes and acorn squash until tender, but not brown.

Add the chicken stock and reduce by 1/4. Add all but 1/4 cup of the fish stock and reduce by 1/3. Purée 2/3 of the crawfish meat and add the remaining fish stock while puréeing. Strain the vegetables and purée. Add back to the chicken stock, along with the crawfish purée and fish stock.

Add the heavy cream. Season to taste and simmer for 15 minutes.

Cut the corn off the cob. Dice and blanch the remaining potatoes. Cut the zucchini into thin strips. Dice the remaining crawfish and return everything to the soup. Garnish with crushed pecan pieces.

YIELD: 1 1/2 GALLONS

Chef Michael Deihl,
Anna's Beachside Café

1/4 cup clarified
  butter*
1 1/2 Vidalia onions,
  diced
5 stalks celery, diced
1/2 pound carrots,
  diced
1/2 cup pecan pieces
1 pound potatoes,
  peeled and diced
1 1/2 acorn squash,
  peeled and diced
16 cups chicken stock**
4 cups fish stock**
1 pound crawfish
  meat, cooked
3 cups heavy cream
3 roasted ears of corn
1 pound potatoes
1 small zucchini
1/4 cup crushed pecan
  pieces
salt, white pepper and
  cayenne pepper to
  taste
*See glossary.
**May substitute
canned broth, bouillon
or water.

21

Bell Pepper Soup with Crab Meat & Chives

3 cups Vidaila onion, chopped

2 teaspoons finely chopped garlic

2 teaspoons finely chopped shallots

1/2 cup unsalted butter

3 cups chopped red pepper

3 cups chopped yellow pepper

1/2 cup White Port wine

3 cups heavy cream

2 cups chicken stock*

1 pound lump crab meat

1 tablespoon chopped chives

Salt and pepper to taste

* May substitute canned broth, bouillon or water.

Sauté half the onion, garlic, shallots in half the butter in one pot until translucent. Repeat in another pot. Add red bell peppers to one pot and yellow bell peppers to another pot. Add 1/4 cup of Port wine to each pot and simmer until reduced by half. Add 1 1/2 cups of cream to each pot and reduce until thick. Purée soups separately and pass through a fine strainer (keep separate) and add chicken stock and simmer to correct consistency.

To serve, use two 3-ounce ladles and pour soup into bowl at the same time. Garnish with warm lump crab meat and chopped chives.
SERVES 6

*Sous Chef Bill Ryan,
Westin Resort*

22

Boniato and Roasted Garlic Soup

Boil Boniato until tender to a fork, purée it with the roasted garlic. Add all ingredients to the stock except the cream. Cook at a rapid boil for 35 minutes, add the cream and thicken with the roux (a mixture, usually equal parts of flour and butter, cooked slowly over a low heat, used to thicken the soup).
SERVES 30-40

4-6 Boniato (Cuban sweet potatoes)
15-20 roasted garlic cloves
4 quarts stock, meat based*
1 cup shredded Asiago cheese**
8 tablespoons minced shallots
2 leeks, julienned
1 quart heavy cream
salt and pepper to taste
2 cups of roux

*May substitute canned broth, bouillon, or water.

**See glossary.

*Chef Aaron Glugover,
Lagniappe*

Bread Soup with Italian Sausage and Chévre Cheese

1 pound crusty Italian bread, several days old
1/2 pound mild Italian sausage
1/2 pound unsalted sweet butter
3 large garlic cloves, minced
8 large sage leaves, fresh and minced
1/2 pound all purpose flour
1 1/2 pounds Roma or vine-ripe tomatoes, small dice
1 1/2 quarts chicken or beef stock (boiling) *
1 pound Chévre (goat) cheese
1/2 quart heavy cream
salt and freshly ground black pepper to taste

*May substitute canned broth, bouillon, or water.

Cut bread into 1" cubes. Cook sausage in stock pot over medium heat. Stir and break-up sausage and cook until done. Pull from stove, strain off excess grease. Heat butter in pot and add the garlic and sage. Sauté over medium heat for 5 minutes. Add sausage and flour, mix and stir well and cook for another 5 minutes. Add tomatoes and bread and cook 2 more minutes. Slowly start adding boiling stock while stirring vigorously. Bring to a boil and then turn down to slow simmer. Let cook for 15 minutes. Add cheese, stir well. When cheese is well incorporated, pull from stove, cover and let sit for 30 minutes. Add salt and pepper to taste. Lightly re-heat if desired and serve.

SERVES 8-10

Chef Joe Molnar, Antonio's

24

Butternut Squash and Lobster Bisque

Blanch lobsters and remove meat from claws, knuckles, and tails (reserve all shells to make stock). In a large pot sweat 1 onion, carrots and celery in butter over medium heat (do not brown). Add tomato paste, lobster shells, and water. Bring stock to a simmer for 1 hour. Reduce by one third original amount. Coat remaining onion and squash with olive oil and roast in 350 ° oven until squash is fork tender. Remove meat from squash and discard skins. Reserve this meat and roasted onion. Strain stock. In a food processor, puree squash and onions with lobster stock. In a clean pot return this mixture to a simmer and add sugar, salt, pepper, cream and sherry. Let simmer for 15 minutes. Garnish soup with chopped lobster meat and serve.
SERVES 16

2, 1 pound lobsters
  (reserve shells)
2 large onions (rough
  chop)
2 carrots (rough chop)
4 stalks of celery
  (rough chop)
4 ounces butter
1 tablespoon tomato
  paste
3 quarts water
4 butternut squash
4 ounces olive oil
  (extra virgin)
1 tablespoon sugar
salt and pepper to taste
1 pint heavy cream

Executive Chef Boyd Palker,
Hyatt Regency Hilton Head

Butternut Squash Soup

4 butternut squash
2 cups heavy whipping
   cream
1 cup chicken stock*
1/8 teaspoon nutmeg
1/8 teaspoon cinnamon
2 teaspoons salt
2 teaspoons white
   pepper
2 tablespoons lemon
   juice
2 tablespoons brown
   sugar or honey
2 tablespoons maple
   syrup

* May substitute
canned broth, bouil-
lon, or water.

Peel, clean and cube the squash. Boil until very tender. Don't let the water line get below the squash.

Mash the cooked squash with a food processor or a wire whip. Return to the pot and add all of the other ingredients. Cook for 30 minutes. Add water if needed to thin. Adjust the seasoning as needed. More salt will bring out the squashy flavor but be careful, especially if your chicken stock is salty!
SERVES 4

Chef David R. Hawkes,
Corner Market Café

Captain's Fish Chowder

2 cups diced celery
2 cups diced onion
1 pound butter
3 cups chopped firm
  fresh fish (such as
  mahi-mahi)
1/2 cup white wine
2 cups clam juice
2 quarts heavy cream
8 ounces flour for
  roux
seasoning to taste

Sauté celery and onions in 1/2 pound of butter until onions are clear and celery softens. Add fish chunks and cook 2 minutes longer stirring often. Add wine and braise until fish is done. Add clam juice and cream.

For roux, melt remaining butter in heavy pan, add flour stirring constantly. Cook over medium heat until golden brown. Remove from heat. Set aside to cool. Add roux to soup stirring constantly until well blended. Adjust seasonings. Cook slowly over medium heat until chowder is nice and thick.
SERVES 8-10

Ray Broman,
Captain's Seafood

Calibogue Red Seafood Stew

1 cup olive oil
1/4 cup garlic, minced
1 cup yellow onion, 1/2" dice
2 cups red, yellow and green peppers, 3/4" dice
1 pound peeled and deveined shrimp
1/2 pound scallops
1/2 pound peeled crayfish tails
1/2 pint clams, shucked or canned
1/2 pound your choice boneless, skinless fish chunks
1/2 gallon marinara sauce
1 quart diced tomatoes with juice
1 quart Port wine
1/2 gallon fish stock or clam juice
1/2 cup fresh lemon juice

Lightly sauté garlic in olive oil. Add onions and peppers and stir until glossy in appearance. Add shrimp, scallops, crayfish tails, clams and fish, gently tossing until all begins to cook. Add marinara, tomatoes and Port. Stir to combine. Add fish stock or clam juice and all seasonings.* Stir, allow to reach beginning of boiling point, adjust down to simmer and allow to cook slowly for five minutes.

(continued next page)

28

(continued from previous page)

Add lemon juice and oysters and gently stir until all oysters curl. Add crab, spinach and basil, stir to combine and serve at will. If desired, keep adding your choice of seafood and liquid as needed, it just gets better! Serve with crusty bread.
SERVES 30

Seasonings:
1 tablespoon Old Bay seasoning
1 tablespoon Cajun blackening seasoning
1 tablespoon Jamaican Jerk seasoning
1/4 cup Worcestershire sauce
1/4 cup green Tabasco pepper sauce
1 teaspoon ground black pepper
1 tablespoon oregano leaves, dried
4 bay leaves
1 teaspoon crushed fennel seeds
1/2 cup granulated sugar
1 teaspoon ground cloves

1 pint shucked oysters and liquor
1 pound cleaned claw or lump crabmeat
1 handful steamed fresh spinach leaves, chiffonade*
2 handfuls steamed fresh basil leaves, chiffonade*

*See glossary

Chef Al Walbrecker
Crowne Plaza Resort

29

2 medium onions,
   diced 1/4"
1 red pepper, diced
   1/4"
1 green pepper, diced
   1/4"
1 jalapeño pepper,
   minced
3 cloves garlic, minced
1/4 pound butter
3 tablespoons chili
   powder
1/4 teaspoon cumin
1/4 teaspoon black
   pepper
1 tablespoon salt
dash cayenne pepper
3/4 cup flour
2 quarts chicken
   stock,* cold
3 cups sour cream
1 lemon
2 limes
12 corn tortillas, cut
   into matchstick
   strips

* May substitute
canned broth, bouil-
lon, or water.

Chicken Tortilla Soup with Lemon Lime Creme Fraîche

In a heavy pot sauté the vegetables with the butter and seasonings for 5 - 10 minutes on medium heat, stirring to prevent browning. Stir in the flour and cook for 1 - 2 minutes until the mixture releases from the pot. Using a wire whisk, gradually add the chicken stock. Cook on low-medium heat for 15 - 30 minutes whipping throughout. Slowly, whip in 2 cups sour cream, reserving 1 cup for the creme fraîche. Adjust the seasonings to your desired taste.

For the creme fraîche, zest and mince the lemon and lime into a pan with their juice and reduce by 1/2. Cool and add to the remaining sour cream. Season with salt and pepper and set aside.

Fry the tortillas in 300° oil until crisp. Remove to a paper towel and season with salt and pepper. Serve the soup topped with the tortillas and a dollop of the creme fraîche.

YIELD: 2 QUARTS

Chef John Soulia,
Belfair Country Club

Chilled Apple Soup

8 golden apples,
    quartered
12 ounces dry white
    wine
4 ounces apple juice
4 ounces sugar
1 cinnamon stick
2 large slices of
    gingerroot
4 ounces sour cream
4 ounces heavy cream
lemon juice, as
    needed

Combine apples, wine, 1/2 the apple juice, sugar, cinnamon and gingerroot; bring to a boil. Simmer mixture until apples are tender. Remove cinnamon and gingerroot. Pureé the mixture. Blend the sour cream and heavy cream, and add to apple pureé. Adjust consistency with remaining apple juice. Chill soup thoroughly. Adjust seasoning with a few drops of lemon juice.
SERVES 8

Aaron Hatfield,
Crane's Tavern

Chilled Georgia Peach Soup

1 quart water
12 ounces granulated
    sugar
10 fresh peaches (may
    substitute 12 ounces
    canned peaches)
16 ounces orange juice
2 ounces Amaretto
    liquor (optional)
2 ounces cornstarch
8 ounces cold water
1 tablespoon ground
    nutmeg
1 bunch fresh mint
    leaves

Bring water to a boil and stir in sugar until dissolved. Add peaches (with syrup if using canned) return to boil, reduce heat to simmer and cook until peaches are a soft mush consistency. Strain liquid to remove pits. Return liquid and as much peach pulp to original container. Hold while completing remaining procedures. Bring orange juice to a boil in a separate pot, reduce to simmer, add liquor (optional). Blend cornstarch and cold water, stir cornstarch slurry to make a smooth creamy paste. Add slurry to simmering orange juice, whisk until thickened. Simmer mixture for 5 minutes. Combine with first mixture and blend well. Add nutmeg to season. Pour into a clean container. When partially cooled, refrigerate. Serve in chilled bowl. Garnish with mint leaf. Serve on a hot summer day, and enjoy!
SERVES 12

Chef Paul Pinski,
Café at Belfair

Christmas Eve Oyster Chowder

Melt the butter in a large soup pot. Add the onion and celery. Cook, stirring occasionally until soft. Add the potatoes, carrots, parsley and 2 cups of half-and-half. Simmer, uncovered for 15 minutes or until the potatoes are tender. Stir in the corn and the remaining cup of half-and-half, sugar, pepper and salt.

The chowder may be refrigerated overnight at this point, if desired. Before serving, add the oysters with their juice. Simmer 5 - 8 minutes, or until the oysters' edges curl.

Serve immediately with oyster crackers.
SERVES 8

4 tablespoons butter
1 large onion, chopped
2 celery stalks, chopped
2 potatoes, peeled and chopped into 1/2" cubes
2 medium carrots, peeled and sliced into 1/4" cubes
1/4 cup chopped parsley
3 cups half-and-half
17-ounce can creamed style corn
1/2 teaspoon sugar
1/4 teaspoon freshly ground pepper
1 teaspoon salt, or to taste
1 pint oysters with juice

Dotti Trivison, Food Editor
The Island Packet

33

Crab and Corn Chowder

6 ounces melted butter
1 large onion, diced
1 stalk celery, diced
1 teaspoon garlic,
  chopped
6 ounces flour
4 ounces sherry
1, 28 ounce can clam
  juice
1, 48 ounce can cream
  corn
1 quart heavy cream
1 gallon milk
4 baking potatoes,
  diced
1 pound crab meat
  picked clean
salt and pepper to taste
2 tablespoons dill weed

In a 12 quart stock pot, sauté onion, celery, and garlic in butter until tender, approximately 3 minutes, stirring regularly so all cook evenly. Add flour and whisk to make a roux; cook 4 minutes, whisking continuously so as not to burn. Deglaze with sherry. Add remaining liquids and potatoes, cook 45 minutes to 1 hour. Add crab and season with salt, pepper and dill weed.
YIELD: ABOUT 3 GALLONS

Chef John Cowen,
The Boathouse II

34

Crayfish and White Bean Ratatouille

Heat the olive oil and add the shallots, garlic and onion. Sauté until tender.

Add the white beans, 1/2 the crayfish, fish stock and heavy cream. Simmer for 1 hour and purée.

Sauté the remaining vegetables until they are 1/2 cooked and add to the puréed soup mixture. Season to taste. Dice the remaining crayfish and add to the soup mixture. Simmer for 1 hour. SERVES 10

2 tablespoons olive oil
1 tablespoon shallots, minced
1 tablespoon garlic, minced
1/4 cup sweet onion, diced medium
1 cup cooked white beans
1 cup crayfish
*1 quart fish stock**
1 quart heavy cream
6 tablespoons zucchini, diced medium
6 tablespoons bell pepper, diced medium
6 tablespoons yellow squash, diced medium
salt and white pepper to taste

* May substitute canned broth, bouillon, or water.

Chef Michael Deihl,
Anna's Beachside Café

Cream of Mussel Soup

5-6 pounds mussels
2 cups dry white wine
1/2 cup chopped
  shallots
3 tablespoons chopped
  fresh parsley
1 teaspoon fresh thyme
2 cups heavy cream
3 large egg yolks
salt and pepper to taste
1/2 teaspoon curry
  powder
fresh chives and
  scallion for garnish

Scrub the mussels under cold running water, remove the beards, discard any with broken shells or those that do not close with a sharp tap on the counter. Another way to know the good mussels is choose those that feel heavy for their size. Use mussels the day they are gathered or bought. NOTE: to obtain the best flavor from the mussels, wash and strain the cooking liquid very well through a coffee filter, paper towel or cheese cloth.

Place in a large soup pot the mussels, wine, shallots, and herbs. Cover and steam over medium heat until all the mussels are completely open. Discard any that do not open. Strain the cooking liquid very well into a medium saucepan, bring to a low simmer, do not boil. Meanwhile, remove the mussels from their shells and reserve.

Mix together the cream and the egg yolks in a small bowl. Gradually whisk about 1 1/2 cups of the cooking liquid into the egg mixture, then whisk back into the saucepan. Do not boil or it will break. Season with salt and pepper and the curry, garnish with the chives, scallion and the reserved mussels.
SERVES 8

Chef Cesar Gonzales,
Primo!

Cream of Potato Soup with Shrimp and Fresh Basil

Heat the olive oil in a heavy saucepan over medium heat. Add the onion, garlic and bay leaf and sauté for 5 minutes. Add the stock and potatoes and simmer for 10 minutes or until the potatoes are cooked.

Melt the butter in a large heavy skillet over medium heat. Add the shrimp and sauté for 2 minutes. Remove from heat. Add the brandy and ignite with a match. When the flames subside, return the shrimp to heat and sauté for 2 minutes or until the shrimp is cooked. Add the shrimp to the soup. Add the whipping cream to the soup and bring to a boil. Season with salt and pepper to taste. Add the fresh basil.

To serve, ladle the soup into eight bowls, evenly distributing the shrimp.
SERVES 8

Chef Mehdi Varedi,
Cattails

3 tablespoons olive oil
1 onion, chopped
2 cloves garlic,
   chopped
1 bay leaf
5 cups fish stock* or
   clam juice
3 medium potatoes,
   peeled and diced
1 tablespoon butter
1 pound small shrimp,
   uncooked, peeled
   and deveined
4 tablespoons brandy
1 cup whipping cream
1 teaspoon salt
1/4 teaspoon white
   pepper
1 tablespoon
   chopped fresh basil

* May substitute
canned broth, bouil-
lon, or water.

Cream of Three Mushroom Soup

2 ounces dried porcini
mushrooms
1 cup + 3 ounces
brandy
3 tablespoons butter
1 cup chopped onions
2 cups oyster
mushrooms
2 cups button
mushrooms
1 quart chicken stock
or broth*
1 teaspoon dried
thyme
1 cup heavy cream
salt and pepper to
taste

* May substitute
canned broth, bouil-
lon or water.

Soak porcini mushrooms in 1 cup brandy for 30 minutes. Lightly sauté onions in butter for 10 minutes. Add oyster and button mushrooms and cook for 10 minutes. Add 1/2 quart of chicken stock, thyme and porcini mushrooms and simmer for 20 minutes. Cool slightly and puree mixture roughly. Return to stove top; add heavy cream, remaining stock, remaining brandy. Season with salt and pepper to taste.
SERVES 6

*Chef Michael Polese,
Formerly of Okatie Creek Restaurant,
Sun City Hilton Head*

Four Onion Soup

Heat the butter. Add the onions, leeks, scallions, shallots and garlic. Sauté until golden brown then add the flour. Mix well and brown slightly. Add the stock and the next 5 ingredients. Bring to a boil. Simmer for 30 minutes. Add the ginger and adjust seasonings to taste.
SERVES 10

3 tablespoons unsalted butter
2 cups yellow onions, sliced
2 cups leeks, sliced
2/3 cup scallions, sliced
1/3 cup shallots, minced
1 1/2 tablespoons garlic, minced
1 1/2 tablespoons flour
7 cups chicken stock*
pinch of cayenne pepper
1 cup cognac
1 1/2 tablespoons lemon juice
salt to taste
freshly ground black pepper to taste
2 tablespoons ginger, minced

*May substitute canned broth, bouillon or water

*Chef Michael Sigler,
Sigler's Rotisserie and Seafood*

39

Frogmore Stew

1/4 cup vegetable oil
4 tablespoons butter
2 cups diced onion
2 cups diced red bell
  pepper
2 cups diced green bell
  pepper
1/2 pound andouille
  sausage
1/2 cup flour
2 gallons fish stock,
  clam juice, or clam
  base*
10 new potatoes,
  quartered
4 ears corn, cut into
  3/4" cobbletts
1 pound shrimp,
  21/25 count
1 pound scallops,
  U-15
1 pound crab meat or
  claws

*May substitute
canned broth, bouil-
lon or water

Sweat onions and peppers with sausage in fat. Dust with flour, cook for 2 minutes, do not brown the flour. Add stock and remaining ingredients, including all seasonings.* Simmer until potatoes and seafood are done.
SERVES 6

*Seasoning:
1 teaspoon thyme
1 teaspoon oregano
1 teaspoon black pepper
cayenne pepper to taste
kosher salt to taste
1 tablespoon Old Bay seasoning

*Executive Chef Edward Allen,
Westin Resort*

"Gary Dee's" Shrimp Bisque

In a food processor, finely chop the celery, onion, pepper, garlic and parsley. Place in a soup pot with the olive oil.

Grind the shrimp to a paste in the food processor and add to the chopped vegetables.

Add the brandy to the soup pot and allow to cook until the shrimp and vegetables are done. Add the heavy cream, half-and-half and milk to the mixture. Bring to a boil, then allow to simmer. Add salt and pepper to taste. Add roux to thicken if necessary. Garnish with paprika.
SERVES 6

4 sticks celery
1 small onion
1 small red bell pepper
1/2 teaspoon chopped garlic
3 sprigs parsley, chopped
1/4 cup olive oil
3/4 pound medium shrimp, peeled and deveined
1/2 cup brandy
1 quart heavy cream
1 pint half-and-half
1 pint whole milk
salt and white pepper to taste
1/4 cup roux* to thicken
1 teaspoon paprika

* See glossary.

Chef Gary Williams,
The Sea Shack

41

Gazpacho

6 cucumbers peeled, seeded and diced
1 green and 1 red bell pepper, seeded and diced
5 cups tomatoes, peeled and diced
1 medium onion, peeled and diced
1/2 cup chopped cilantro
1 lime, juiced
1 jalapeno, diced
1 quart tomato juice
2 garlic cloves, minced
1/4 cup red wine vinegar
3 teaspoons ground cumin
1 tablespoon ground New Mexican chili *
1 tablespoon Worcestershire Sauce
dash of Tabasco pepper sauce
salt and pepper

* May substitute any chili powder.

Combine all ingredients and process in pulses to achieve a chunky style. Process this mixture longer in processor or blender for a smooth style. Chill and serve.
SERVES 24

Executive Chef Jon Gilliam,
Café Europa

42

Lawson's Black-eyed Pea Gumbo

In a large sauce pan, brown chicken, shrimp and sausage. Add olive oil, and next four ingredients. Cook over medium heat until celery softens. Add flour, cook 1 minute, stir slowly. Add stock and cook 10 minutes. Add crushed tomato, white corn, okra and black-eyed peas. Season to taste.* Simmer 15 to 20 minutes stirring often. Serve around hot cooked white rice. Garnish liberally with chopped chives.
SERVES 10 - 12

*Seasonings:
chopped garlic
salt and pepper
thyme
oregano
hot sauce
Worcestershire sauce
chives

8 ounces chopped chicken
1/2 pound medium shrimp
8 ounces chopped sausage
6 tablespoons olive oil
4 bay leaves
1/2 cup onion
1/4 cup diced celery
1/4 cup diced bell pepper
1/3 cup flour
1 cup pork or chicken stock*
1/2 cup crushed tomato
1/2 cup white corn
1/2 cup okra
2 cups black-eyed peas

* May substitute canned broth, bouillon, or water.

Chef Brad Terhune
Captain's Seafood

43

Lowcountry Bouillabaisse

1 ounce olive oil
1 cup yellow onion, minced
1 tablespoon garlic, minced
2 cups fresh fennel, diced
2 cups white wine
pinch of saffron
1 ounce dried oregano
1 ounce dried basil
4 cups diced tomato, canned
1 cup tomato sauce
1 can small diced clams
6 soft shell crabs
1 cup lobster meat, cut into large chunks
1 cup peeled and deveined shrimp, small
1/2 pound fish, such as swordfish, mahi-mahi, or catfish, cut into large chunks
season to taste with salt and pepper

In a large sauce pot, sauté onion, garlic and fennel until tender. Add wine, herbs, tomatoes. Simmer sauce for 20 minutes. Add clams and wait until they begin to open, then add the rest of the seafood. Serve in a large bowl or platter for your guests to choose from. Serve with French bread or any sour dough bread. Note: Add fish stock or clam juice or water to keep "brothy" if the dish reduces too much; also, clams and shrimp will release natural juices.
SERVES 6

Chef Gerald Bruck,
Crown Plaza Resort

44

New England Clam Chowder

Sauté bacon, onion and celery. Add salt and pepper. Remove from stove. Boil potatoes in two cups of water until soft. Add remaining ingredients and cook 20 minutes over medium heat, stirring occasionally. If thicker chowder is desired add a simple roux of equal parts cooked butter and flour. SERVES 10

6 slices bacon, diced
3 small onions, diced
2 medium potatoes, diced
24 ounces clams, drained and diced
4 cups milk
2 cups heavy cream
1/4 cup margarine
2 teaspoons salt
1/2 teaspoon white pepper
1/2 teaspoon celery salt

Chef Marty Pellicci
Crazy Crab Harbour Town

New York Cheddar and Ale Soup

6 cups mirepoix :
(3 cups onion, 1 1/2
cups carrot, 1 1/2 cups
celery, all chopped)
1 1/2 tablespoons
garlic, minced
3/4 pound butter, divided
1 1/2 cups flour, divided
12 cups chicken stock*
1 1/2 bottles ale or
dark beer
1 tablespoon Lawry's
Seasoned Salt
2 teaspoons white pepper
1 tablespoon Tabasco
pepper sauce
3 tablespoons
Worcestershire sauce
2 tablespoons Dijon
mustard
1 1/2 cups sharp
cheddar cheese, grated
2 cups cream
1 red pepper, finely diced
1 green pepper, finely diced

*May substitute canned
broth, bouillon, or water.

Sweat* the mirepoix and garlic in 1/2 cup of the butter.

Make a roux with 1 cup of the butter and 1 cup of the flour. Cool the roux. Process the cooked mirepoix and garlic in a food processor.

Boil the following in a large pot: chicken stock, beer, salt, pepper, Tabasco, Worcestershire sauce and mustard.

Whip the cooled roux into the boiling mixture. Add the mirepoix to the roux and the boiling liquid (velouté).

Toss the grated cheese in the 1/2 cup of flour. Over a low heat add the cheese, cream and peppers to the soup, stirring constantly. Simmer for 15 - 20 minutes.

YIELD: 1 GALLON

* See glossary.

Chef Steve Hancotte,
Stripes

Oyster and Roasted Corn Chowder with Fried Leek Julienne

Render fat from diced bacon in stock pot. Add diced onions and celery and sweat until tender. Add roasted corn kernels and toss with other vegetables. Add oyster liquor (juice of oysters) and reduce by one-third. Add heavy whipping cream and bring to a boil. Reduce heat and simmer for 15 minutes. Add uncooked diced potatoes. Add shucked oysters. Thicken soup with roux* to desired consistency. Season with salt, pepper, thyme, and Tabasco pepper sauce. Garnish soup at service with parsley, if desired. YIELD 1/2 GALLON

Sous Chef James Campbell
The Westin Resort

1/2 cup bacon, small dice
1/4 cups onions, medium dice
1/2 cup celery, medium dice
2 cups corn kernels, roasted
2 cups oyster liquor (juice of oyster)
2 cups heavy whipping cream
1 cup russet potatoes, peeled, medium dice
1 cup oysters, shucked (save liquid)
Roux*
To Taste: salt, ground black pepper, chopped fresh thyme, Tabasco pepper sauce

Garnish (Optional)
Parsley, Chopped

*See glossary

Polenta Soup

4 tablespoons olive oil
4 ounces Prosciutto
   ham, small dice
2 medium red onions,
   small dice
3 celery stalks, small
   dice
3 medium carrots,
   small dice
4 tablespoons tomato
   paste
salt and freshly ground
   black pepper to taste
3 quarts + 1 cup
   chicken stock *
1/2 pound coarsely
   ground yellow
   cornmeal

* May substitute
canned broth, bouillon
or water.

Heat olive oil in stock pot. When hot, add the Prosciutto and sauté for 5 minutes. Add vegetables and cook for another 5 minutes. Add tomato paste, stir well, then season with salt and pepper. Add 1 cup chicken stock and cook for 10 minutes, stirring occasionally.

Add remaining 3 quarts of chicken stock and bring to a boil. Slowly start adding the cornmeal in a steady stream. Stir continually with a flat wooden spoon, being sure no lumps form. When all of the cornmeal is added, lower the heat and simmer for 45 minutes, stirring occasionally.

Taste soup. Adjust seasonings. Serve. Sprinkle with olive oil.
SERVES 8-10

Chef Joe Molnar
Antonio's Restaurant

48

Portobella Mushroom, Duck, and Andouille Sausage Gumbo

Roast the ducks and pull off the meat. Sauté the trinity (green pepper, celery and onion) until tender. Add everything to stock except roux and cook for at least two hours. Add dark roux and thicken to desired consistency. Serve with filé powder.
SERVES 30-40

2 whole ducks
2 green peppers
1 bunch celery
1 large onion
6 tablespoons garlic, minced
6 tablespoons shallots, minced
10 portobella mushrooms, rough chop
6 andouille sausage, sliced thin
4 quarts meat based stock *
salt and pepper to taste
2-4 cups dark roux **
filé powder **

* May substitute canned broth or bouillon.
** See glossary.

*Chef Aaron Glugover,
Lagniappe*

49

Roasted Garlic New Potato Soup

1/2 pound bacon
3 stalks celery
3 onions
6 heads garlic
   (not cloves)
1/4 cup oil
1/2 pound flour
2 quarts chicken broth *
1 quart half-and-half
1 tablespoon thyme
3 large red potatoes,
   blanched and diced

* May substitute canned broth or bouillon cube.

Dice and render bacon. Dice celery and onion, add to rendered bacon. Sauté 2 minutes. In a separate pan, trim tops off garlic heads, oil, cover and bake at 350 ° until tender (40 minutes). Add flour to bacon pot, stir well. Add chicken broth, stir well. Add half-and-half; simmer. Remove garlic from oven, let cool slightly and squeeze roasted garlic from skin. Stir into soup. Add thyme and blanched diced potatoes, simmer 10 minutes more. Eat and enjoy!
SERVES 12

Chef Tom Egerton,
Crane's Tavern

Roasted Tomatillo with Blackened Scallops Soup

Combine tomatillo, onion, and garlic in a roasting pan, sprinkle with salt and pepper and roast at 350 ° for approximately 1 hour. Remove from oven and combine with chicken stock in a soup pot, bring to a boil, add tequilla and lime juice. Check for salt and pepper.

Coat scallops in seasoning and sear the scallops in a cast iron skillet. Float on top of soup. SERVES 4

2 1/2 pounds tomatillos, peeled
1 onion, diced
2 tablespoons garlic, chopped
salt and pepper to taste
1 cup chicken stock *
1/4 cup tequila
2 tablespoons lime juice
12 medium scallops
1/4 cup blackening spice

* May substitute canned broth or bouillon.

Chef Brad Blake,
Sunset Grille

51

Sausage Corn Chowder

4 pounds link sausage
(any flavor)
4 dozen ears of sweet
corn
1/2 pound butter
1 large onion.
chopped fine
1 cup flour
2 large potatoes.
cubed
2 quarts chicken
stock*
1 quart heavy cream
1 quart milk
salt and pepper

*May substitute
canned broth, bouil-
lon or water.

On the grill cook sausage, then let cool. Now husk and rinse corn and grill enough to lightly put grill marks on the corn, let cool. In a large pot add butter and onion, cook until translucent. Cut sausage into small cubes and cut corn from the ear. Put into the pot and cook 5 minutes. Now add flour, let cook 5 minutes, constantly stirring. Add potatoes, chicken stock, cream and milk and bring to a boil stirring. Once thickened add salt and pepper to taste.
YIELD: 20 SERVINGS

Chef Nick Anderson,
Just Pasta Café

Seared Scallop and Oyster Stew

In a medium saucepan, heat 1 tablespoon of the olive oil over high heat, add the shallots and cook until tender. Add the wine and reduce by 1/2. Once reduced, add the heavy cream and reduce by 1/3, about 5 minutes. Remove from the heat and add the crumbled pasilla pepper and allow to steep for 10 minutes.

In a medium saucepan, over high heat, reduce the clam and oyster juices by 1/2. Meanwhile, place the pepper/cream mixture into a blender and purée until smooth. Strain through a fine sieve into the clam juice pan while discarding pasilla scraps. Adjust the seasoning of the broth to taste with salt and white pepper. Keep warm over a low heat.

Heat a large teflon-coated sauté pan over high heat and add the remaining olive oil. Season the scallops with salt and white pepper. Carefully add the scallops to the hot pan, so that they do not overlap. Cook until well seared, about 1-3 minutes, quickly turning the scallops until done. Add the oysters and peppers and cook until just heated.

(continued on next page)

2 tablespoons olive oil
2 shallots, finely chopped
1 cup dry white wine
1 cup heavy cream
1 dried pasilla pepper,* stemmed, seeded and crumbled
2 cups clam juice
2 dozen oysters, shucked, reserving the oyster juice
salt to taste
white pepper to taste
1/4 pound large scallops
1 roasted red pepper, finely diced
1 roasted yellow pepper, finely diced
1 tablespoon fresh tarragon, chopped
1 tablespoon parsley, chopped

* See glossary.

53

(continued from previous page)

While cooking the scallops, return the clam broth to a boil. Equally divide the scallops, peppers, and oysters among 4 hot soup bowls. Carefully ladle the hot clam broth into the bowls. Sprinkle with chopped tarragon and parsley and serve.

SERVES 4

Chef Keith Josefiak,
Starfire

She-Crab Soup

Sauté onion and celery in butter. When translucent, add flour. Cook over low heat for approximately five minutes. Add all other ingredients except crab meat. Simmer 20 minutes. Add crab, and adjust seasonings.

1 1/2 GALLONS

Chef Michael Sigler,
Sigler's Rotisserie and Seafood

1 onion diced
2 celery ribs, diced
4 ounces butter
4 ounces flour
salt and white pepper
1 tablespoon crab
   base*
   (may substitute
   chicken base)
Mace to taste
6 ounces Harvey's
   Bristol Cream
1/2 gallon milk
3 pints heavy cream
1 pound backfin crab
1 pound crab claw
   meat
1/2 pound blue
   crab roe
   (may substitute
   ground carrot)

Sachet Bag:
1 teaspoon fennel seed
1 bay leaf
1 teaspoon peppercorns
parsley stems

* See glossary.

Shrimp and Sausage Gumbo

1 stalk celery
2 yellow onions
1/2 cup oil or butter
2 pounds smoked
  sausage
2 pounds shrimp
1 pound frozen corn
1 pound okra - frozen
1 #10 can crushed
  tomatoes = 6, 16
  ounce cans
1, 46 ounce can V-8
  juice
1 quart water
1 cup rice
1 teaspoon cayenne or
  to taste
1/2 cup sugar
1/4 cup chicken base*

*See Glossary.

Chop celery and onion and place in large pot with heated oil or butter. Cook 3 minutes. Add sausage and shrimp. Sauté 2 minutes. Add corn, okra, tomatoes, V-8 juice and water. Bring to a boil for about 5 minutes. Lower heat and simmer 20 minutes. Add rice, cayenne, sugar and chicken base. Simmer for 10 minutes. Serve.
SERVES 20

*Chef Gwendolyn C. Bynum,
Reilly's North - Port Royal Plaza*

Study of Shellfish (Bouillabaisse Method)

In a heavy gauge pot, heat oil and add vegetables, except potatoes. Add garlic and shallots. Sauté until onions are translucent, add shrimp and scallops. Add potatoes and sauté for additional 2 minutes. Add fish stock, white wine, Old Bay seasoning and saffron, bring to simmer, cook until potatoes are fork tender. Add crawfish, lobster meat and crab claws.

Simmer for 3 minutes, adjust seasonings to taste. Place one crab claw in each bowl, distribute remaining bouillabaisse equally between each bowl. Serve with crusty French bread.
SERVES 6-8

Executive Chef Nick Totten,
Old Fort Pub

3 tablespoons oil
1 cup carrot, peeled
   and diced
2 medium onions,
   diced
1 cup diced and
   seeded tomato
1 cup celery, diced
1 tablespoon garlic,
   minced
1 tablespoon shallots,
   minced
1/4 pound shrimp,
   peeled and cleaned
1/4 pound sea scallops
2 potatoes, peeled and
   medium dice
1 quart + 2 cups fish
   stock *
2 cups white wine
2 teaspoons Old Bay
   seasoning
A pinch of saffron
1/2 pound crawfish
   tails (cleaned)
1/2 pound lobster
   meat, diced
1 or 2 clusters of snow
   crab claws
2 tablespoons salt and
   pepper
French Bread
   (optional)

* May substitute
canned broth, bouillon,
or water.

57

Salads

2

Artichoke Salad

Make a court bouillon* and cook the scallops. Cool immediately. Add the remaining ingredients with the scallops to a mixing bowl. Toss and refrigerate. Serve on a shell dish garnished with leaf lettuce.
SERVES 20

* See glossary.

Chef Robert C. Montbleau
Formerly of Port Royal Clubhouse

3/4 pound scallops
8 red peppers, julienned*
2 white onions,
 julienned
1 yellow pepper,
 julienned
3 red onions,
 julienned
4 large tomatoes, diced
50 Greek olives
1 bunch parsley
 (optional)
1 bunch basil
5, 10-ounce cans
 artichoke hearts,
 halved
1/2 cup garlic, minced
1 bunch tarragon
3 tablespoons red
 pepper, crushed
2 tablespoons salt
juice of 2 lemons
1/2 cup vermouth
3 tablespoons black
 pepper
1/2 cup olive oil
pinch of saffron
*See glossary.

Cornmeal Crusted Calamari Salad

1 pound calamari
2 cups yellow cornmeal
1 cup all-purpose flour
kosher salt
cracked black pepper
ground cayenne pepper
2 cups fresh spinach
1 cup feta cheese,
   crumbled
1/2 cup kalamata
   olives
3/4 cup Mediter-
   ranean Vinaigrette.*

*See under Salad
   Dressings.

Clean the calamari and cut into 1/4" rings. Mix the cornmeal, flour and seasonings. Toss with the calamari. Sift, and lightly fry at 325°.

Toss the spinach with the feta cheese, olives and the Mediterranean Vinaigrette. Top with the crispy calamari.

SERVES 4

Chef Paul Colella,
The Captain's Table

Curried Chicken Salad

In a large bowl, combine the chicken, cashews, celery, green onion, apple and raisins. Blend the chutney, mayonnaise, curry and lemon juice and combine with the chicken mixture. Season to taste with the cayenne and garlic salt. Add additional curry if desired. Chill.

Serve in the prepared melon halves and garnish with a small bunch of green grapes.
SERVES 4

3 cups cold, poached chicken, shredded
1/2 cup cashews, coarsely chopped
2 stems celery, diced
2 tablespoons green onion, chopped
1 green apple, cored and diced
2 tablespoons raisins
2 teaspoons chutney
3/4 - 1 cup mayonnaise
2 teaspoons curry powder
2 teaspoons lemon juice
cayenne pepper to taste
garlic salt to taste
2 cantaloupes, halved, seeded and fluted*
bunch of green grapes

* See glossary.

Chef Deborah Van Plew

63

24 ounces chicken breast (6 four-ounce breasts)
2 tablespoons curry
1 tablespoon vegetable oil
3 tablespoons diced apple
2 tablespoons shredded coconut
1 tablespoon red onion, diced fine
2 tablespoons olive oil
salt and pepper to taste
1 cup balsamic vinegar
1 seedless cucumber
1 carrot
1 yellow tomato
12 slices French bread
3/4 tablespoons garlic, chopped
1 tablespoon olive oil
salt and pepper
6 ounces goat cheese

Curried Chicken Salad with Apple, Coconut, Balsamic Vinegar and Goat Cheese Croutons

Marinate chicken breasts with curry and vegetable oil, one to two hours. Cook chicken at 375° for 10-12 minutes or until done. Cool chicken and julienne. Mix chicken with apples, coconut, onions and olive oil and season. Reduce balsamic vinegar on high heat to 3/4 its volume and cool. Cut 40 thin slices of cucumber. Line mold with sliced cucumber. Place on plate and fill with curried chicken salad and press down. Make peels with carrots and fry crisp. Julienne yellow tomato. Place fried carrots and julienne of tomato on top of mold; drizzle with reduced vinegar. Brush French bread slices with garlic, olive oil, salt and pepper. Bake at 400° for 5 minutes. Remove; spread goat cheese on top and bake again for 2 minutes. Place around salad.
SERVES 6

Executive Chef John Briody,
Colleton River Plantation

English Stilton with Walnut Salad

Slice the radicchio and romaine lettuce into julienne* strips. The spinach and endive should remain in whole leaves. Coarsely chop the walnuts and crumble the Stilton cheese. Lay the spinach and endive leaves (3 per portion) on each serving plate. Arrange the other ingredients on top. Mix all of the ingredients for the dressing and serve over the top of the salad.
SERVES 4

*See glossary.

Chef Gerard Thompson

1 head radicchio
  lettuce*
1/2 head romaine
  lettuce
12 leaves spinach
1 head endive
8 tablespoons walnuts
4 tablespoons Stilton
  cheese
8 yellow pear toma-
  toes, cut into wedges

Dressing:
6 tablespoons balsamic
  vinegar
1/2 cup walnut oil
1 teaspoon parsley,
  chopped
1 teaspoon red onion,
  finely diced
1 teaspoon watercress,
  chopped
1 teaspoon salt and
  pepper
1/2 teaspoon garlic,
  chopped

* See glossary.

Grilled Portobella Mushrooms over Mixed Greens

1 cup teriyaki sauce
1/4 cup orange juice
1/4 cup sesame oil
4 large portobella caps

1/2 cup red wine
  vinegar
1/2 cup balsamic
  vinegar
3/4 cup sugar
1 teaspoon Dijon
  mustard
2 cups salad oil
1/4 cup sundried
  tomatoes, chopped
1/4 cup basil, chopped

1 cup mixed greens
1 cup fresh mozzarella
1 large tomato, cut
  into 8 wedges

Mix the teriyaki sauce, orange juice and sesame oil in a bowl and marinate the portobella mushroom caps for 3 - 5 hours.

To prepare the sundried tomato basil vinaigrette, mix together the red wine vinegar, balsamic vinegar, sugar, Dijon mustard and salad oil. Mix in the sundried tomatoes and the basil.

To assemble the salads, divide the greens, cheese and tomatoes into 4 portions. Grill the mushrooms until hot all the way through. Slice and top the salads with the mushrooms and the vinaigrette.

SERVES 4

Chef Paul Pinski,
Café Belfair

66

Grilled Portobella Mushroom Salad

To prepare the marinade, mix together 1/4 cup of the olive oil, Worcestershire sauce, balsamic vinegar, red wine vinegar, soy sauce, 1 tablespoon of the chopped garlic, 1 tablespoon of the shallots, rosemary, and salt and pepper. Marinate the portobella cap for 1 hour.

Grill the portobella cap, upside down first, turning once. Cook until tender (5 - 7 minutes). Top with the lump crab and goat cheese and toast under a broiler.

To prepare the raspberry vinaigrette, combine the remaining olive oil, garlic and shallots with the mustard, sugar, raspberry vinegar , and salt and pepper to taste.

Mix the raspberry vinaigrette with the greens and arrange on a cold plate with the portobella cap on top. Sprinkle with chives and freshly cracked black pepper.
SERVES 1

Chef Keith Tanenbaum,
Alligator Grille

3/4 cup olive oil, divided
1/4 cup Worcestershire sauce
2 tablespoons balsamic vinegar
2 tablespoons red wine vinegar
1/4 cup soy sauce
2 tablespoons garlic, chopped, divided
2 tablespoons shallots, chopped, divided
2 tablespoons fresh rosemary
salt and pepper to taste
1/4 cup lump crabmeat
2 tablespoons goat cheese
2 tablespoons Dijon mustard
2 tablespoons sugar
1/4 cup raspberry vinegar
salt and pepper to taste
1/2 cup mixed greens
chives

Mista Salad

Equal amounts of:
1 bunch baby spinach
1 bunch arugula, cored
1 small head radicchio,
*   sliced & cored*
1 bulb fennel hearts or
*   2 - 3 stems, sliced*

Clean and stem spinach, arugula, radicchio and fennel. Slice the radicchio and fennel. Toss all with balsamic vinaigrette (recipe follows). Finish with roasted peppers of choice and freshly shaved Romano cheese, or Insalata di Tonno which follows.

Balsamic Vinaigrette: 1 part balsamic vinegar to 2 parts extra virgin olive oil. Add fresh chopped garlic, basil, oregano, salt and pepper to taste. Mix well.
SERVES 4

Chef Francesco Scotto,
Trattoria la Spiaggia

Insalata di Tonno

12 ounces tuna

4 red bell pepper

Grill tuna to preferred degree of doneness. Roast red peppers ahead. Cool, peel, slice, and set aside. Place 3 ounces tuna on top of equal amounts of Mista Salad; top with roasted bell peppers. Voila!

SERVES 4

Chef Francesco Scotto,
Trattoria la Spiaggia

Roasted Charleston Chicken Salad

3 pounds boneless
  chicken breasts,
  skin-on (about 6 - 8
  breasts)
1 tablespoon mesquite
  seasoning
1 1/2 cups mayonnaise
1/4 cup honey
1 tablespoon whole
  grain mustard
6 stalks celery, diced
1/2 cup pecan pieces,
  toasted
salt and pepper to
  taste

Rub the chicken breasts with the mesquite seasoning. Arrange the breasts on a lightly oiled sheet pan and bake in a 375° oven for approximately 15 minutes. Remove the chicken and cool.

To prepare the dressing, mix the mayonnaise, honey and mustard. Add the celery and pecans.

Remove and discard the skin from the breasts. Dice the chicken into 1/2" pieces and mix well with the dressing. Add salt and pepper to taste.

Serve chilled on a lettuce leaf with garnishes of your choice.

SERVES 8

Executive Chef Jon C. Gilliam,
Café Europa

Roasted Vegetable Pasta Salad with Fresh Shrimp

Preheat the oven to 350°. To prepare the dressing, combine the mustard, oil, lemon juice, garlic, salt and black pepper. Toss the peppers and eggplant in the mixture. Place in a pan and roast for 20 - 25 minutes. Let cool.

Toss with the pasta and shrimp.
SERVES 2 - 4

2 tablespoons Dijon
  mustard
1 tablespoon olive oil
1 tablespoon lemon
  juice
2 garlic cloves, minced
1/4 teaspoon salt
1/8 teaspoon black
  pepper
1 red pepper,
  julienned*
1 green pepper,
  julienned
1 eggplant, julienned
3/4 cup rotelle* pasta,
  cooked
1/2 pound of 16-20
  count shrimp, cooked
  and chilled

* See glossary.

*Chef Jimi Sundling,
The Kingfisher*

Sautéed Shrimp and Steamed Vegetable Salad

3 to 4 heads baby
  lettuce
1/2 cup wild
  mushrooms
2 tablespoons oil
50 shrimp, peeled and
  deveined
salt and pepper to
  taste
1 bulb fennel,
  julienned*
3 large leeks,
  julienned*
1 large carrot,
  julienned*
1 large onion,
  julienned*

Vinaigrette:
1 clove garlic, chopped
12 basil leaves,
  chopped
1 large tomato, peeled,
  seeded and diced
juice of 1 lemon
1 cup peanut oil
*See glossary.

Clean the lettuce and wild mushrooms, then set aside. Heat the oil in a large sauté pan. Add the shrimp and season to taste. Sauté the shrimp until pink and firm. Remove and set aside. Steam the julienned vegetables and wild mushrooms for 3 to 5 minutes. Remove from the steamer and allow to cool.

Whisk together the garlic, basil, tomato and lemon juice in a bowl. Slowly whisk in the peanut oil and season to taste. Arrange the lettuce on a serving plate and place the steamed vegetables in the center. Top with the shrimp and lace with the vinaigrette.
SERVES 10 - 12

*Chef Jim McLain,
Callawassie Island*

72

Shrimp and Avocado Acapulco

Peel, seed and dice the avocados. Cover with orange juice and set aside. (This prevents discoloration, but does not alter the flavor.)

To prepare the simple syrup, also called a sugar syrup, combine the sugar and water and cook over a low heat until clear, then boil for about a minute. This syrup can be flavored with liqueurs, extracts and juices. Combine with the next 8 ingredients. Dress with the lemon juice and oil. Season to taste. Make a cup on the plate with the radicchio and Boston leaves. Place the shrimp salad in the center of the lettuce cup. Garnish with citrus zest. Drain the orange juice from the avocado cubes and place the avocado around the remaining salad.
SERVES 12

Former Executive Chef Brian Tess, The Westin Resort

6 avocados
orange juice
1/2 cup sugar
1 cup water
1 pound shrimp, 51 count, poached, peeled and chilled
1 red onion, finely diced
1 bunch green onions, finely cut
2 cups jicama,* peeled and cut into 1/4" sticks
7-8 tomatoes, cubed
2 green bell peppers, diced
1 teaspoon cilantro
1 tablespoon basil leaves, julienned*
1/4 cup lemon juice
1/2 cup salad oil
salt and white pepper
cayenne pepper to taste
12 radicchio leaves
12 hearts of Boston lettuce leaves
1/2 cup zest (orange, lemon and lime)
* See glossary.

White Bean Salad

1 cup dried white northern beans, soaked in water overnight and drained
2 teaspoons dried thyme
1 bay leaf
1/4 cup olive oil
1 tablespoon fresh rosemary, minced
3 cloves garlic, minced
1/4 cup yellow onion, diced
1/4 cup red bell pepper, roasted, peeled, seeded and diced
2 tablespoons balsamic vinegar
1 tablespoon red wine vinegar
2 tablespoons parsley, chopped
salt to taste
freshly ground black pepper to taste

In a large pot, combine the white beans, thyme and bay leaf. Add cold water to cover and bring to a boil over medium-high heat. Reduce heat to low and simmer for about 2 hours, or until the beans are tender. Remove the bay leaf and drain. Allow beans to cool to room temperature.

In a large sauté pan, over high heat, warm the olive oil until just smoking. Add the rosemary and garlic and cook until golden brown and aromatic. Add the onions, reduce the heat to low, and cook until tender, about 10 minutes. Transfer to a large mixing bowl. Add the beans, red pepper, balsamic vinegar, red wine vinegar and parsley. With a mixer attachment, mix on low speed until the mixture is just combined and beans are slightly mashed. Do not overmix. Season with salt and pepper to taste.

Refrigerate until ready to use. Best served at room temperature. Thin with a little warm water if mixture becomes too thick. Serve with assorted crackers and crusty breads.
SERVES 4

Chef Keith Josefiak,
Starfire Contemporary Bistro

Wild Field Greens with Grilled Portobella Mushrooms

Brush the mushrooms lightly with olive oil, salt and pepper. Place on a hot grill, turning once, until tender. Remove, cover and set aside.

To prepare the vinaigrette, in a small bowl, whisk the garlic, mustard and vinegar together. Season with salt and pepper to taste. Drizzle in the oil in a slow, steady stream, whisking constantly until the dressing is creamy and thickened and all the oil has been incorporated. Correct the seasonings as needed. Makes about 1 1/2 cups. Set aside.

Place the washed and dried field greens in a large bowl, pour on just enough vinaigrette to gently coat the greens, not smother them. Toss lightly and sprinkle with the pine nuts and Gorgonzola. Toss again and place on individual plates. Cut the mushrooms in half and into thick slices. Divide and fan out over the top of the greens.

SERVES 6

Dotti Trivison, Food Editor
The Island Packet

3 large portobella caps
1 cup, plus 2 table-spoons extra-virgin olive oil
salt and freshly ground black pepper
1 garlic clove, pressed
1 tablespoon Dijon mustard
3 tablespoons balsamic vinegar
8 cups mixed wild field greens (mesclun)
2 tablespoons pine nuts
3 tablespoons Gorgonzola cheese, crumbled

Salad
Dressings

Balsamic Vinaigrette

Add the first 5 ingredients in a mixing bowl
and stir together. Slowly fold in the oil.
YIELD: 21 OUNCES

1 cup balsamic
   vinegar
1 cup brown sugar
2 teaspoons basil
1 teaspoon salt
1 teaspoon white
   pepper
1/2 cup olive oil

Chef Scott Allen,
Scott's Fish Market

Creamy Garlic and Herb Salad Dressing

8 cups mayonnaise
1/2 cup vinegar
2 tablespoons
  Parmesan cheese,
  grated
1/2 teaspoon sweet
  basil
1/2 teaspoon thyme
1/2 teaspoon oregano
1/2 teaspoon black
  pepper
4 1/2 teaspoons garlic
  powder
3 cups milk

Combine all of the ingredients in a large mixing bowl. Mix until well blended. Let stand for about 15 minutes. Taste and adjust the seasoning if necessary. The dressing may thicken as it sets. Thin it down with milk, if desired.

YIELD: 3 QUARTS

Chef Michael J. Zornouski,
Formerly of the Westin Resort

80

Creamy Gorgonzola Salad Dressing

Mix all of the ingredients very well in a stainless steel bowl and refrigerate. Will keep for 7 - 10 days.

YIELD: 1 QUART

3 1/2 cups Gorgonzola
  cheese, crumbled
1 cup mayonnaise
1 1/2 tablespoons
  coarse black pepper
1 tablespoon fresh
  garlic, minced
1 tablespoon fresh
  shallots, minced
1 tablespoon
  Worchestershire
  sauce
1 tablespoon Dijon
  mustard
1 cup sour cream
1 1/4 cups cream
2 teaspoons Lawry's
  seasoned salt
2 tablespoons fresh
  chives, chopped
1/2 cup half-and-half

Chef Steve Hancotte,
Stripes

1 3/4 teaspoons ginger
  purée
1 1/4 teaspoons garlic,
  chopped
1 1/4 teaspoons fresh
  dill, chopped
1/4 bunch fresh
  parsley, chopped
1 1/4 teaspoons dried
  basil
1 1/2 tablespoons
  kosher salt
2 1/2 teaspoons black
  peppercorns, crushed
1 1/2 tablespoons
  granulated sugar
5 teaspoons whole
  grain mustard
5 teaspoons
  lemon juice
1/2 cup red wine
  vinegar
3 1/4 tablespoons
  tarragon vinegar
6 tablespoons olive oil
2 cups peanut oil

Ginger Vinaigrette

Mix all of the ingredients together except the oils. Stir well to dissolve the sugar and salt. Add the oils and mix well.

YIELD: 1 QUART

Chef Rick Stone,
Formerly of Rick's Place

Jamaican Jerk Marinade

Finely mince the garlic and onion using a food processor. Whisk together with remaining ingredients and coat the item to be marinated overnight. Grill over hot coals, basting with the marinade.

YIELD: 20 OUNCES

1/2 tablespoon garlic, minced
1 small yellow onion, minced
1/4 tablespoon chili peppers, crushed
1/2 tablespoon cracked black pepper
1 tablespoon ground cardamom
1 tablespoon ground nutmeg
1/2 tablespoon ground cinnamon
1/2 tablespoon ground clove
3 tablespoons dried thyme
1 1/2 cups tamarind paste (substitute with Lea & Perrins)
1/4 cup Key lime juice (can be bottled)
1/4 cup corn oil

Chef William Henry IV,
The Westin Resort

3/4 cup balsamic
   vinegar
1/4 cup lemon juice
dash of white wine
   vinegar
dash of Tabasco pepper
   sauce
1 tablespoon fresh
   garlic, minced
2 cups extra virgin
   olive oil
salt and pepper to taste

Mediterranean Vinaigrette

Combine the first five ingredients. Slowly add the olive oil while whisking the vinegar. Season with salt and pepper.
YIELD: 3 CUPS

Chef Paul Colella,
The Captain's Table

84

Scallion Vinaigrette

Blanch the scallions in a pot of boiling water until tender, about 1 minute and drain well. In a blender, combine the scallions, mustard, chopped parsley and vinegar. Purée until smooth. With the blender running, slowly add the clam juice and olive oil. Continue to purée until well emulsified. Adjust the seasoning and strain the vinaigrette through a fine sieve into a small bowl. Reserve at room temperature.

YIELD: 1 1/2 CUPS

5 scallions, trimmed of root
2 tablespoons Dijon mustard
3 tablespoons parsley, chopped
1/4 cup white wine vinegar
3/4 cup clam juice
1/4 cup olive oil
salt
white pepper

Chef Keith Josefiak,
Starfire

85

Walnut Vinaigrette

1/2 cup sherry vinegar
1 teaspoon honey
1 teaspoon Dijon
  mustard
1 whole shallot,
  finely chopped
1 teaspoon coarse black
  pepper
1 tablespoon parsley,
  chopped
1/2 teaspoon thyme,
  chopped
1/4 teaspoon garlic
  chopped
1/2 teaspoon salt and
  pepper
1/2 cup walnut oil
1 1/2 cups grape seed
  oil
2 tablespoons hot
  water

In a medium mixing bowl, add the vinegar, honey, mustard, shallot, black pepper, parsley, thyme, garlic, salt and pepper. Whisk in the oils slowly. Add water until incorporated. Store in a bottle and refrigerate.

YIELD: 3 CUPS

Former Executive Chef Brian Tess,
The Westin Resort

Appetizers

Artichoke Hearts and Crabmeat Sauté

Melt the butter and add the artichoke hearts, crabmeat, lemon juice, vermouth and shallots. Bring to a boil for one minute. Add the parsley and scallions.

Place the artichoke mixture over the spinach and serve.

SERVES 4

1/2 stick butter
10-ounce can artichoke hearts, chopped
8 ounces fresh crabmeat
3 tablespoons lemon juice
2 tablespoons vermouth
1 tablespoon shallots, minced
2 tablespoons parsley, chopped
2 tablespoons scallions, minced
1/2 bag of spinach, washed & shredded

Chef Johnny Highberger
Formerly of High Z's

Artichoke Heart Fritters

20 artichoke hearts
1 egg
pinch of sugar
pinch of salt
pinch of pepper
4 tablespoons cream
1/4 cup beer
1/4 cup water
1 cup flour
2 cups oil

Wash and clean the artichoke hearts and pat dry with a towel. Set aside. Combine the egg and the following six ingredients. Blend with a wire whisk until the batter starts to thicken. Adjust the thickness by adding water slowly. Do not over dilute.

Dredge the artichoke hearts in the flour and place in the batter, coating thoroughly. Heat the oil in a heavy skillet. Place the fritters in the oil and cook all sides approximately 3 minutes or until golden brown. Remove and pat dry with a towel. Season with salt and pepper.

SERVES 4

Chef Geoffrey Fennessey,
The Kingfisher

Asian Style Crabcakes

Pick the crabmeat and set aside. Mix the remaining ingredients together except for the breadcrumbs and sesame oil. For the bread crumbs, make a mixture of 1 part flour to 5 parts bread crumbs. Add the crabmeat and the breadcrumbs and combine well. Form the crabmeat mixture into 1 3/4 ounce balls. Form the crab balls into cakes about 2 inches in diameter. Sauté over high heat in the sesame oil. Drain on paper towels and serve with the Mango Beurre Blanc.

To prepare the Mango Beurre Blanc, combine the wine, vinegar and shallots in a nonreactive saucepan and reduce by 2/3 over a medium heat. Add the heavy cream and reduce by 1/2. Cut the cold unsalted butter into cubes and incorporate it into the liquid mixture adding only 2 tablespoons at a time and whisk. Add the mango purée and the basil. Keep warm.

Note: the temperature of the mixture is critical when adding the butter. About 105° is a good temperature.
SERVES 10

Chef Rick Stone,
Formerly of Rick's Place

4 pounds lump crabmeat
1 bunch cilantro, chopped
6 ounces fermented black
 beans, rinsed and drained
1 bunch scallions, chopped
2 cups celery, chopped
2 cups bean sprouts,
 lightly chopped
4 cups carrots, grated
2 tablespoons hot bean paste
2 tablespoons chopped garlic
2 tablespoons ginger purée
2 tablespoons fish sauce
1 tablespoon oyster sauce
6 eggs
3 cups Japanese breadcrumbs
sesame oil

Mango Beurre Blanc:
1 cup white wine
1/2 cup rice vinegar
1 tablespoon shallots, chopped
1/4 cup heavy cream
1 pound unsalted butter
1/4 cup mango purée
2 tablepoons fresh basil,
 julienned*
* See glossary.

91

1 French baguette,
sliced and toasted

Tartare:
2 ounces red bell
pepper, brunoise*
4 green onions,
chopped
1 teaspoon garlic,
chopped
1 teaspoon gingerroot,
peeled and grated
1/4 cup soy sauce
1/4 cup rice wine
vinegar
8 ounces tuna, small
dice
2 tablespoons honey
2 tablespoons sesame
oil
salt and pepper,
if necessary

*See glossary

Asian Tuna Tartare with Cucumber and Daikon Kim Chee

Quickly sauté the peppers, onions, garlic and ginger. Deglaze with soy sauce and vinegar, and cool completely. Gently toss the mixture with the tuna, and season with honey and sesame oil. Add salt and pepper if necessary.

(continued on next page)

(continued from previous page)

For the Kim Chee: Combine all ingredients, reserving sesame seeds for garnish. Place in a sealable container, and chill for 3 days, if possible. Otherwise, gently press vegetables, and allow the mixture to marinate for two hours. Then chill and serve.

SERVES 4

Kim Chee:

1 cup Napa Cabbage, chiffonade*

1 1/2 cup Daikon* or radish, julienned*

1 1/2 cup cucumber, peeled and julienned

1 teaspoon garlic, chopped

2 teaspoons gingerroot, grated

2 hot, red chile (2" long); split

1/2 teaspoon paprika

1/4 cup rice wine vinegar

1/4 cup soy sauce

1/2 cup water

2 tablespoons honey

1/4 cup black and white sesame seeds

*See glossary

Chef Paul Colella,
Captain's Table

Basil Grilled Shrimp St. John

2 tablespoons fresh basil
1 tablespoon pine nuts
1 clove garlic
2 tablespoons olive oil
1 tablespoon fresh
  Parmesan
salt and pepper to taste
24 medium - large
  shrimp, peeled and
  deveined
4 wooden skewers

Dressing:
1 cup raw bacon, diced
1/4 cup onion, diced
1/4 cup white wine
  vinegar
1/4 cup brown sugar
1/2 teaspoon black pepper
1 cup sour cream

Parmesan Basket:
2 cups fresh shredded
  Parmesan cheese
1 sheet parchment paper
fresh spinach, picked
  and cleaned
tomatoes, diced

Purée the first six ingredients in a food processor. Skewer the shrimp and rub down with the basil mixture. Set aside until ready to cook.

To prepare the dressing, sauté the bacon on medium heat until crisp. Drain off 1/2 of the fat. Add all of the other ingredients, except the sour cream. Simmer 5 - 10 minutes on medium heat. Reduce heat to low and slowly add the sour cream.

To prepare the Parmesan basket, divide the Parmesan into 4 equal rounds on a lined sheet pan. Spread the cheese evenly. Bake at 350° until golden brown. Let the cheese cool 1- 2 minutes. Mold the cheese over a small bowl or coffee cup and let cool.

To assemble, grill the basil shrimp. Toss the spinach in the warm dressing and place in the Parmesan basket. Top with the shrimp and tomatoes.

SERVES 4

Chef John Soulia,
Belfair Country Club

94

Carolina Bayou Smoked Gator Stuffed Shrimp

Combine the basil, butter and honey for the marinade and glaze the gatormeat while warming the smoker. Then smoke for 3 to 5 minutes. Allow the meat to cool.

Peel, devein and butterfly the shrimp, leaving the tails on. Sprinkle lightly with the "Old Bay Seasoning" and butter.

Remove all of the cartilage from the crabmeat. Grind the gatormeat and crabmeat to a hamburger consistency and set aside. Combine all of the remaining ingredients and sauté until soft. Drain and add to the gator and crabmeat mixture. Stuff the shrimp with the filling and dust lightly with the flour. Bake at 375° for 8 to 10 minutes.
SERVES 100

Chef Gary D. Williams,
The Sea Shack

1/4 cup basil, chopped
1 stick butter
1 cup honey
2 pounds gator tail
    meat
5 pounds (51-60
    count shrimp)
Old Bay seasoning*
butter
1 pound lump
    crabmeat
6 cups saltine crackers,
    crushed fine
8 eggs
6 medium shallots,
    minced
1/2 cup brandy
1/2 stalk celery, minced
2 medium carrots, diced
1 large onion, diced
salt and pepper
Tabasco pepper sauce
4 tablespoons
    Worcestershire sauce
1 cup heavy cream
3 cups flour

*See glossary.

95

2 regular size sheets
  puff pastry dough
1/4 cup flour
1 small bunch parsley,
  finely chopped
4-6 large shrimp
4-6 large scallops
1, 6-ounce lobster tail,
  shelled
1 stick butter
1/4 cup dry white
  wine
salt and pepper
1 egg (for egg wash)
1 to 1 1/2 cups heavy
  cream
roux*
dash of Pernod
pinch of dill

* See glossary.

Carolina Seafood Biscuits with Pernod

Thaw the puff pastry at room temperature. Place on a lightly floured surface and sprinkle on the chopped parsley. Cut 24 circles out of the dough using a medium cookie cutter.

Cut the seafood into small pieces. Preheat the sauté pan. Add the butter, then the seafood and white wine. Sauté for 2-3 minutes. Salt and pepper to taste. Place the seafood on the circles of dough. Top each with another circle of dough and seal it with an egg wash. Bake at 350° until brown.

Meanwhile, in a saucepan, mix the leftover juice from the seafood with the cream, and bring to a boil. Make a roux from the remainder of the flour and butter. Salt and pepper to taste. Thin with the cream mixture. Add the Pernod for flavor and the dill for color. Spoon the sauce over the biscuits and serve.

SERVES 4

Chef Gary D. Williams,
The Sea Shack

96

Chèvre Stuffed Mushrooms

Clean the mushrooms, separating the caps and stems. Set the caps aside. Chop the following into small pieces: mushroom stems, onion, green pepper and red pepper. In a large skillet, sauté the chopped vegetables and the garlic in olive oil. Add the fennel seed and crumbled bacon. Continue to sauté until the vegetables are tender. Remove from the heat. Fold in the chèvre cheese and the Parmesan cheese. Let the mixture stand for at least one hour to combine the flavors. Stuff the mushroom caps with the cheese mixture and broil until the caps are tender.

YIELD: 3 DOZEN

3 dozen large mushrooms
1 small onion
1 green pepper
1 red pepper
1 teaspoon garlic, minced
2 tablespoons olive oil
1 1/2 tablespoons fennel seed
3/4 cup bacon, cooked and crumbled
12 ounces chèvre cheese*
1/4 cup Parmesan cheese, grated

* See glossary.

Chef Scott Miller
Formerly of Charlie's

97

Country Paté

5 pound boneless pork
  butt
1 pound pork liver
3-4 garlic cloves
1/2 pound onions
5 sprigs parsley
2/3 cup flour
4 eggs
2 tablespoons salt
pinch of curing salt
1/2 teaspoon ground
  pepper
2 tablespoons brandy
1/2 pint heavy cream

Grind finely the following: 2 pounds of pork meat, pork liver, garlic, onion, and parsley. Grind the remaining meat coarsely. Place all of the ingredients in a mixing bowl, beat slowly, adding the flour, eggs, seasoning, brandy and heavy cream. Place the mixture in a terrine.* Cook in a water bath* in a 325° oven until done.

Refrigerate overnight. Serve with thin slices of warm toast and garnish with cornichons.*
YIELD: 10 - 12 slices

* See glossary.

Chef Geoffrey Fennessey,
The Kingfisher

Crab Cakes

Mix crab, onion and 3/4 cup of crackers. In another bowl, beat eggs. Add milk, Worcestershire sauce, salt, pepper and mustard. Form into small, individual cakes. Dredge in remaining crumbs. Heat oil in skillet to medium high. Sauté until golden grown turning once, about 4-5 minutes per side.
SERVES 4

1 pound claw crabmeat
1 cup green onion, chopped
1 1/2 cups Ritz crackers, crushed
2 eggs
1/4 cup milk
1 teaspoon Worcestershire sauce
salt to taste
1/2 teaspoon pepper
1 tablespoon Dijon mustard
oil

Chef Marty Pellicci,
Crazy Crab Harbour Town

Crab Savannah

3 teaspoons butter, softened
1 teaspoon Italian
 seasoning
4 slices French bread
8 medium button mush-
 rooms, quartered
8 shittake mushrooms,
 stems removed, and
 julienned
4 teaspoons capers
1 teaspoon garlic, chopped
1 teaspoon shallots,
 chopped
4 tablespoons olive oil
1/2 cup dry sherry
1 cup fish stock*
1/2 cup heavy cream
corn starch
1/2 teaspoon fresh
 thyme, chopped
8 ounces lump
 crabmeat, shells removed
1 cup tomatoes, diced
salt and pepper
1/2 cup Parmesan cheese
1 tablespoon parsley
4 lemon wedges
* See glossary.

Mix the butter and Italian seasoning together and spread on one side of the French bread.
Toast the bread in a 250° oven until crisp.

In a medium-sized sauté pan, sauté the mushrooms, capers, garlic, and shallots with olive oil for
2 minutes, being careful not to burn the garlic and
shallots. Deglaze* the pan with the sherry. Add the
fish stock and heavy cream. Bring to a boil and
tighten the mixture with corn starch until a thick
sauce consistency is reached. Add the fresh thyme,
crabmeat, diced tomatoes, salt and pepper to taste.
Place the French bread slices in individual casserole dishes and spoon the mixture over the top of
them. Sprinkle with the shredded Parmesan cheese
and brown under the broiler. Garnish with the
chopped parsley and lemon wedges. Serve immediately.
SERVES 4

* See glossary.

Chef Clarke Murdough,
Formerly of Hemingway's at the Hyatt Resort

Crabmeat Beignets

Sift together dry ingredients (flour, salt, soda, Old Bay) and set aside. Whisk eggs and half-and-half together. Slowly add egg mixture to dry mixture until fully incorporated. Blend in crab, pepper and onions. Drop teaspoon size balls of mixture into hot oil (350°) and fry for 3 minutes. Turn and fry an additional 2 minutes. Drain and serve with red pepper jelly, cocktail sauce, or tartar sauce. SERVES 12

3 cups all purpose
flour
1 teaspoon salt
1 teaspoon baking soda
2 tablespoons Old
Bay seasoning
4 eggs
1 cup half-and-half
1 pound lump
crabmeat
1/4 cup fine diced bell
pepper
1/4 cup fine minced
green onion

Chef Richard Vaughan,
Spartina Grill

4 tablespoons butter
4 tablespoons flour
1 1/2 cups milk
6 egg yolks
7 egg whites
1/2 cup Gruyère
    cheese, grated
4 tablespoons
    Parmesan cheese
salt and pepper

Easy Cheese Soufflé

Melt the butter in a saucepan, adding the flour. Boil the milk and add to the flour mixture. Grease an 8" soufflé dish and dust with the flour or grated Parmesan cheese. Preheat the oven to 375°. Incorporate the egg yolks one by one, mixing well after each addition. Add the cheese and season to taste. Beat the egg whites to a stiff peak. Fold carefully into the cheese mixture. Fill the soufflé dish to 1" under the rim and bake for 35 minutes. SERVES 2

Chef Geoffrey Fennessey,
The Kingfisher

Fried Tofu with Lemon Coriander Sauce

This traditional Thai appetizer is a simple 3-step way to prepare light and delicious vegetarian food. Serves two as a main course or four as an appetizer.

Reserve 1 1/2 cups canola oil in a small non-reactive bowl. Reserve 1/2 cup coriander and rough chop; add this to reserved oil; add smashed lemon, shallots, pepper, salt. Stir and leave at room temperature.

Heat remaining oil to 375° in large wok or deep wide pot. Fry tofu until golden brown in batches of 2 so the oil stays hot.

Place warm tofu on shredded cabbage and spoon on the sauce. Garnish with coriander leaves and serve with chopsticks.

SERVES 4

1/2 gallon canola oil for frying
1 1/2 cups Thai coriander leaves or cilantro
2 lemons smashed with a cleaver
1 small shallot, diced
2 heaping teaspoons crushed, mixed peppercorns
1 heaping teaspoon kosher salt or more, to taste
1 pound package of firm organic tofu, sliced horizontally into eighths
2 cups shredded Napa cabbage

Shawn Luedtke & Peggy Abbott, proprietors
Taste of Thailand

6 prawns
1/2 cup fresh tomatoes,
diced
1 tablespoon fresh
garlic, minced
2 tablespoons sweet
chili sauce
1 tablespoon whole
butter
2 tablespoons scallions

Grilled Prawns with Tomatoes, Scallions and Sweet Chili

Grill the prawns until tender and set aside. In a sauté pan, sauté the tomatoes and garlic for 30 seconds. Add the sweet chili and whip in the whole butter. Serve over the grilled shrimp. Garnish with the scallions. Serve over basmati rice.
SERVES 1

Chef Keith Tanenbaum,
Alligator Grille

Grilled Tuna Cakes with Grilled Georgia Peach Chutney

Brush tuna with olive oil and season with salt and pepper. Grill over a high flame until just cooked. Set the tuna aside and allow to cool. In a large bowl, combine all other ingredients and mix well. With a fork, flake the cooled tuna into the bowl and fold in. Adjust seasonings. Form into cakes. Season the flour with salt and pepper. Dust tuna cakes with seasoned flour and sauté in olive oil over high heat. Drain them on a paper towel and arrange on serving plate with the peach chutney.

To prepare the peach chutney, peel, half and core the peaches. Combine all of the ingredients in a heavy bottomed sauce pan. Allow peaches to marinate for 30 minutes. Remove the peaches and grill. Over a medium heat, cook the remaining ingredients for 30 minutes, stirring often. Dice the peaches and add to the liquid. Let cool.
SERVES 4

Chef Brian Stockholm
Formerly of Rick's Place

1 pound yellowfin tuna
2 tablespoons olive oil
1/2 cup flour
4 tablespoons red onion, diced
3 tablespoons capers
2 tablespoons cornichons,* diced
4 tablespoons fresh dill, minced
2 tablespoons olives, diced
3 tablespoons mayonnaise
2 tablespoons Dijon mustard
Chutney:
6 cups peaches
1/2 cup yellow onion, minced
4 tablespoons ginger, minced
1 1/2 cups red peppers, finely diced
1 cup brown sugar
1 cup sugar
6 tablespoons rice wine vinegar
1 vanilla bean
*See glossary.

Jumbo Lump Crab Cockta with Citrus Cucumber Vinaigrette

1 lemon
1 lime
1 orange
3/4 cup of white balsamic vinegar
1 teaspoon fresh chopped garlic
1 teaspoon fresh chopped shallot
1 tablespoon sugar
1 hot house cucumber, seeded
1/2 cup extra virgin olive oil
salt and pepper to taste
1 pound fresh picked jumbo lump crab meat
1 each red, yellow and green pepper diced (for garnish)
4 flat bread crackers (optional)
4 chilled plates

Vinaigrette:

In a mixing bowl squeeze the juice of the lemon, the lime and the orange into the bowl, add the vinegar, garlic, shallot and sugar. Puree the cucumber in food processor, add it into the bowl. Mix with wire whisk while adding the oil in slowly to form an emulsion. Taste the vinaigrette, add salt and pepper as needed.

Presentation:

Toss the crab in the vinaigrette without breaking up the beautiful jumbo lumps. Put the crab centered onto the chilled plates, about 4 ounces on each plate. Sprinkle the diced peppers around the plate then spoon some of the juice on top of the crab and on the plate. Garnish with flat bread crackers.

SERVES 4

Executive Chef Nick Totten, Old Fort Pub

Jumbo Shrimp in Whole Grain Mustard Sauce

5 jumbo shrimp
2 tablespoons clarified
  butter*
1/4 cup sherry
1 teaspoon shallots,
  minced
1/2 cup cream
1 teaspoon whole grain
  mustard
salt and pepper to taste

Peel and devein the shrimp leaving the tails on. Sauté the shrimp in the clarified butter. Remove the shrimp and deglaze* the pan with the sherry. Add the shallots and the cream. Reduce to the desired thickness. Add the mustard and adjust the seasoning.

Serve the shrimp with an angel hair pasta, tossed in butter.

SERVES 1

* See glossary.

See glossary.

Chef/Owner Michael Sigler,
Sigler's Rotisserie

107

2 tablespoons garlic, minced
2 cups assorted mushrooms, finely chopped
1 cup leeks, minced
1/2 cup carrots, minced
1/2 cup celery, minced
1 1/2 cups sherry
2 cups breadcrumbs
1/4 cup fresh parmesan cheese, grated
salt and pepper to taste
4 large wonton wrappers
1 egg, beaten
olive oil

4 tablespoons garlic, minced
6 vine-ripened tomatoes
2 tablespoons olive oil
1 cup sherry
1 pint heavy cream
salt and pepper to taste

Mushroom and Vegetable Ravioli with Roasted Tomato Crème

Sauté the garlic and vegetables. Deglaze with the sherry and reduce by 1/2. Add the breadcrumbs and cheese. Season with salt and pepper. Fill each wonton and fold into a large triangle and seal with an egg wash. Place in boiling water and cook for 3 minutes. Drain and rinse with cold water. Heat the olive oil and sear the ravioli golden brown on both sides.

To prepare the Roasted Tomato Crème, sauté the garlic and tomatoes in the olive oil. Add the sherry and reduce by 1/2. Add the cream. Reduce again by 1/2, and season with salt and pepper.

Top the wontons with the crème sauce and serve.

YIELD: Four 15-OUNCE WONTONS

Chef Paul Colella,
The Captain's Table

Mussels Marinière over Roasted Angel Hair Pasta

Roast the angel hair pasta on a sheet pan in a 400° oven until it starts to turn dark brown, almost burning around the outer edges of the sheet pan. Cook in boiling, salted water until al dente*. (Roasted pasta takes a little longer to cook.) Drain and cool. Blend with olive oil to prevent from sticking together.

To prepare the mussels, sauté in a hot sauté pan with a little olive oil. Add the garlic and shallots. Cook 15 - 30 seconds. Add the white wine, cream, and parsley. As mussels open, remove and reserve them, collecting all of the natural juices in the sauté pan. Reduce by 1/4, then whip in the butter and lemon juice. Serve over the roasted angel hair pasta and garnish with chopped parsley.

SERVES 2

*See glossary

Chef Keith Tanenbaum, Alligator Grille

1 pound dry angel hair pasta
1/4 cup olive oil
30 - 40 Blue Point mussels*
2 tablespoons garlic, chopped
2 tablespoons shallots, chopped
1/4 cup white wine
1/4 cup heavy cream
1 tablespoon fresh parsley, chopped
4 tablespoons butter, softened
1/2 fresh lemon parsley

* See glossary.

2 pounds fresh
  Norwegian salmon
1 1/2 pounds fresh sea
  scallops
juice of 1 lemon
2 tablespoons soy sauce
1/2 teaspoon Tabasco
  pepper sauce
4 tablespoons parsley,
  chopped
6 eggs
1/2 cup heavy cream
salt and pepper to taste
butter

Sauce:
2 tablespoons fresh
  dill, chopped
3 roasted gold bell
  peppers, peeled and
  seeded*
3 cups white wine
1 cup herb butter,
  softened

*May use yellow
peppers.

Oven Steamed Salmon and Scallop Terrine

Preheat the oven to 400°. Fillet the salmon, removing the skin and bones. Put the scallops in a food processor and add the lemon juice, soy sauce, Tabasco, parsley, eggs, and process. Slowly add the cream until blended. Season with salt and pepper.

Thinly slice the salmon. Grease a terrine* with butter. Alternate layers of the salmon and scallop mousse until full. Cover with waxed paper and bake for 25-30 minutes. Remove and set aside.

To prepare the sauce, cut the bell peppers into diamond shapes. Combine with the wine and dill in a sauté pan. and reduce by 1/2. Add the butter, and reduce until creamy. Season with salt and pepper.

Serve slices of the terrine with the warm sauce on top.
SERVES 6 - 8
* See glossary.

Chef Jim McLain,
Callawassie Island

110

Oysters Kilpatrick

Chop the bacon and sauté until brown. Add the onion, garlic, "Season-All" and tomatoes. Sauté until the onions are translucent. Cool for 20 minutes. Add the bread crumbs. Salt and pepper to taste. Place 1-2 tablespoons of mixture on each oyster and bake at 350° until breading is light brown. Serve immediately.
SERVES 8 - 10

3/4 cup bacon, chopped
1 medium onion, diced
2 tablespoons garlic, minced
*3 teaspoons "Season-All"**
4 tomatoes, peeled and finely chopped
6 cups breadcrumbs
salt and pepper
3-5 dozen oysters, shucked

* See glossary.

Chef Geoffrey Fennessey,
The Kingfisher

Pinckney Island Salsa

1 onion, diced
1/2 stalk celery, diced
1/2 jalapeno pepper, minced
1 1/2 green bell peppers, diced
10 plum tomatoes, diced
1 1/2 tablespoons garlic, minced
1/2 cup cilantro, chopped
1/2 teaspoon cumin, ground
1/2 teaspoon salt
1/2 cup corn oil
1/4 cup red wine vinegar
1 1/2 tablespoons Worcestershire sauce
1 1/2 shakes Tabasco pepper sauce
1/2 cup tomato paste

Mix all of the vegetables, herbs and spices, then add the corn oil, vinegar, Worcestershire and Tabasco sauces. Allow to marinate overnight to extract the vegetable juices. Blend in the tomato paste to thicken.

YIELD: 2 Quarts

Chef Dean A. Thomas
Formerly of The Westin Resort

Red Potato Shells with Leeks & Blue Cheese

Saute bacon. In reserved drippings, saute leeks. Toss bacon and leeks with blue cheese, bread crumbs, half-and-half and beaten eggs. Hollow out the potatoes and fill the skins with mixture. Bake at 350° for 12 minutes.

SERVES 8

8 ounces bacon, chopped
2 cups sliced leek
1 1/4 cup blue cheese, crumbled
1 cup dry bread crumbs
1/2 cup half-and-half
2 eggs
24 small 2" red potatoes

*Executive Chef John Briody,
Colleton River Plantation*

Roasted Hazelnut Crusted Fillet of Salmon

1/4 cup roasted hazelnuts, crushed
1/4 cup fresh bread - crumbs
4, 4-ounce salmon fillets
flour for breading
2 eggs, beaten
1/4 cup white wine
1/4 cup cream
1 ounce hazelnut pesto (see below)
1 ounce whole butter
1/2 fresh lemon
salt and pepper to taste

Hazelnut Pesto Sauce:
1 ounce roasted hazelnut
1 1/2 ounces basil
2 tablespoons Parmesan cheese
1 ounce garlic
4 ounces oil
salt and pepper to taste

Mix the roasted hazelnuts and fresh breadcrumbs. Add salt and pepper to taste. Bread the salmon fillets by dusting with flour and dipping in the egg, then crusting with the hazelnut breadcrumb mixture.

To prepare the pesto sauce, blend the hazelnuts, basil, Parmesan cheese, garlic, oil, salt and pepper in a food processor. Set aside.

Sauté the fillets until golden brown and remove from the skillet. Add the wine, cream, and pesto and bring to a boil. Whisk in the whole butter, lemon juice and salt and pepper.

Serve the fillets topped with the Hazelnut Pesto Lemon Crème Sauce.
SERVES 4

*Chef Keith Tanenbaum,
Alligator Grille*

Romaine, Wild Mushroom and Garlic Chive Torte

Butter the entire inside surface of a 9" cheese-cake pan. Blanch the romaine leaves for a few seconds in hot water, then cool. Remove the middle stem from the leaves. Line the pan with the leaves and set aside.

To prepare the filling, combine all of the ingredients (except the sherry) and sauté for about 10 minutes. Add the sherry and cook until most of the liquid is gone. Season to taste and set aside.

Prepare the custard by bringing the milk to a boil. In a bowl combine the remaining ingredients. Whisk until well blended. Whisking continually, slowly add the scalded milk to the egg mixture.

(continued on the next page)

Lining:
1/2 stick unsalted butter
12-14 romaine leaves

Filling:
the following, finely chopped:
1/2 pound mushrooms
2 stalks celery
1/2 large onion
1 1/2 tablespoons fresh basil
1 1/2 tablespoons garlic chives
4 tablespoons oil
1/2 cup sherry

Custard:
4 cups milk, scalded
12 whole eggs, well beaten
1 teaspoon nutmeg
4 teaspoons parsley, chopped

Sauce:

6 medium red bell
   peppers
3 cups water
1 large onion
3 tablespoons oil

(continued from previous page)

By hand, combine the filling with the custard until well blended. Pour into the lined pan. Set the lined pan in a sheet pan half filled with water and bake at 400° for 30-45 minutes.

Prepare the sauce while the torte is cooling. Core, seed, and coarsely chop the bell peppers and boil until soft, then strain. Peel and slice the onion and sauté in the oil until soft. Purée the strained bell peppers with the onion in a food processor until smooth. Strain the purée and season to taste. Pour the sauce onto the plate and place the torte on the sauce and garnish as desired.

SERVES 6

Chef Jim McLain,
Callawassie Island

Smoked Tomato and Jalapēno Salsa

Core and cut tomatoes in half and place in a smoker. Cold smoke* for 45 minutes. In a food processor, blend tomatoes with jalapēnoes, cilantro, tomato paste, sugar, cumin, juice of two limes, and balsamic vinegar. In a pan over low heat, heat olive oil and cracked garlic cloves until cloves are gently browned. Strain out garlic and pour hot garlic oil into tomato mixture. Remove from food processor and pour into mixing bowl. Stir the chopped peppers and onion into the salsa, and season to taste with salt and pepper. Serve with any Southwest style food.

MAKES 1 QUART

*Cold Smoke (low heat 70° - 90°)

Sous Chef William Ryan,
The Westin Resort

5 *ripe tomatoes*
3 *jalapēnoes*
1 *bunch cilantro*
2 *tablespoons tomato*
   paste
1/4 *cup sugar*
1 *teaspoon cumin*
2 *limes*
2 *tablespoons balsamic*
   vinegar
5 *cloves garlic, peeled*
   and cracked
1/2 *cup olive oil*
1 *red pepper, chopped*
1 *green pepper,*
   chopped
1 *yellow pepper,*
   chopped
1 *Bermuda onion,*
   chopped
salt and pepper

Spicy Grilled Jumbo Shrimp on Sweet Potato Haystack

8 shrimp 16/20 count

Marinade:
2 ounces honey
1 ounce key lime juice
pinch of chili powder
pinch of salt and pepper
1 ounce balsamic vinegar
pinch of cayenne

Combine all ingredients and mix well.

1 sweet potato
Oil for frying
2 ounces tomato sauce
1 tablespoon reduced balsamic vinegar
3 fresh chives
1 bud of basil

Marinate shrimp for 10 minutes; grill until done. Julienne sweet potato, fry until crisp; arrange in center of plate; spoon tomato sauce around haystack; place shrimp, tail up, around center; garnish with chives, chopped basil and reduced balsamic vinegar.
SERVES 2

Executive Chef Mike Wallace,
The Hilton

118

Spicy Sesame Ginger Wings

Blend all ingredients except for chicken wings until smooth. Fry the wings until golden brown and coat with sauce. Finish cooking in a hot oven if necessary. Garnish with the toasted sesame seeds.
SERVES A BUNCH

1 tablespoon fresh ginger, minced
2 ounces honey
4 ounces orange juice concentrate
3 ounces Dijon mustard
8 ounces corn oil
8 ounces sesame oil
4 ounces peanut butter, creamy
4 ounces soy sauce
4 ounces chili oil
5 ounces sesame tahini*
8 ounces rice wine vinegar
150 chicken wings
Oil for frying
1 cup toasted sesame seeds

* See glossary.

Sous Chef William Ryan,
The Westin Resort

Torta Rustica

Dough:
4 cups flour
1 teaspoon salt
1/2 pound butter
2 eggs
2 egg yolks
1/2 cup milk

Filling:
30 ounces spinach
1 diced onion
1 tablespoon butter
3 eggs whisked
4 roasted and peeled
   red bell peppers
4 roasted and peeled
   yellow bell peppers
1/2 pound grated
   mozzarella
1/2 pound sliced ham
1 egg beaten with 2
   tablespoons of water

For dough: Combine flour, salt and butter. Mix until flour resembles course meal. Add eggs and yolks, mix. Gradually add milk until dough begins to come together. Gather into a ball, wrap with plastic and refrigerate for one hour.

Blanch and chop spinach. Sauté onions in butter until soft. Add spinach, eggs and season. Roll out 2/3 of the dough and place into springform pan. Layer filling ingredients into the torta (peppers, cheese and ham). Roll out remaining dough, brush with egg wash and fit on top. Bake 40 minutes at 375°.
YIELD: 1 TORTA

Sous Chef William Ryan,
The Westin Resort

120

Entrees

Alligator Chili

Sauté first 3 ingredients. Add beans and alligator sausage. Add rest of ingredients and season. Simmer for two hours. Garnish with crayfish.
SERVES 20-25

1 large onion, diced
2 red and 1 yellow bell peppers, diced
1 cup each pinto beans, red beans, and kidney beans, soaked & cooked off, or canned
3 pounds alligator sausage, diced and sautéed
6 -16 ounce cans/jars marinara sauce
6 large diced tomatoes
1 cup fish stock *

Seasoning:
3 tablespoons chili powder
1/2 cup jalepeno, diced
1 teaspoon curry
1 teaspoon cayenne pepper
salt & pepper to taste

Garnish:
1 pound crayfish, diced

Chef Richard Fausnacht,
Scott's Fish Market

* May substitute canned broth, bouillon, or water .

For the Salmon:
4, 8 ounce fillets fresh
    salmon
salt and pepper

For crust:
3 cups sliced almonds
1/2 tablespoon kosher
    salt
zest of 1 each: orange,
    lemon and lime,
    minced
1/4 teaspoon ground
    white pepper
1/2 teaspoon garlic
    powder
1/2 teaspoon cumin
    powder
1/2 teaspoon powdered
    ginger
1/2 teaspoon onion
    powder
1/4 teaspoon powdered
    nutmeg
1/2 cup honey
1 tablespoon lemon
    juice

Almond Crusted Salmon with a Curry Sauce

Season and sear the salmon. Place aside to cool. Place all ingredients for the crust except honey and lemon juice in a food processor. Pulse until the almonds are about 1/4 inch in size. Place into a bowl and incorporate the honey by hand until the mixture is pliable. If the mixture is too thick, add the lemon juice. In a saucepan, lightly saute the onions with the curry powder for about 2-3 minutes. Add the cream of coconut and orange juice. Bring the sauce mixture to a boil and thicken with the cornstarch slurry until it lightly coats the back of a spoon.

(continued next page)

(continued from previous page)

Spread a thin layer (1/4 inch) of the almond crust over the top of the cooled salmon fillets. Place the topped salmon fillets in a 350° preheated oven for 15-20 minutes or until the fillet has reached an internal temperature of 145 degrees and the crust is golden brown. Ladle sauce around the fillet and garnish with toasted almonds, chopped scallions, and diced peppers.
SERVES 4

For the Sauce:
1 medium yellow
  onion, diced
2 tablespoons
  McCormick curry
  powder
8 ounces cream of
  coconut (Coco
  Lopez)
3 cups orange juice
cornstarch slurry, as
  needed
salt and pepper

Chef Timothy M. Miller,
The Westin Resort

3 pounds Angus beef,
  ground
1 pound veal, ground
1 pound pork, ground
1 1/2 tablespoons coarse
  black pepper
4 carrots, shredded
4 eggs, beaten
2 1/2 cups fresh bread -
  crumbs
1 cup (1/2 bottle)
  ketchup
3 tablespoons
  A.1. Sauce
3 tablespoons
  Worchestershire
  sauce
2 cups yellow onion,
  small dice
2 red peppers, roasted,
  peeled, diced
3 tablespoons fresh
  garlic, minced
1/2 bunch fresh parsley,
  chopped

American Meatloaf

Mix all of the ingredients in a large bowl. Place in 2 glass loaf pans. Place some additional ketchup on top of each loaf. Bake at 350°, in a water bath,* for 2 1/2 hours. Serve with garlic mashed potatoes.

SERVES 8 - 10

* See glossary.

Chef Steve Hancotte,
Stripes

Baked Cobia with Warm Golden Relish

To prepare the relish, chop all of the vegetables in 1/4" pieces. Heat 3 tablespoons of oil in a medium pan set on high. Add the onions and cook until tender. Reduce the heat. Add the flour and stir. Add the remaining vegetables and stir. Add the sugar and the vinegar. Reduce the heat to low, cover, and cook for 20 minutes. Remove the cover and cook for approximately 25 minutes. Salt and pepper to taste. Keep warm while preparing the cobia.

To prepare the cobia, preheat the oven to 350°. Heat the remaining oil in a heavy pan on high. Place the fish, skin side up, in the pan and cook for 1 minute. Turn the fish. Place in the oven and cook 15 minutes. Top with the relish and serve.

SERVES 4 - 6

1 1/2 pounds Cobia*
1 medium onion
2 medium cucumbers, peeled
3 plum tomatoes
1 red pepper, seeded
1 green pepper, seeded
1 yellow pepper, seeded
5 tablespoons olive oil
2 tablespoons flour
2 tablespoons sugar
1/4 cup balsamic vinegar
salt and pepper

* See glossary.

*Chef Richard Canestrari,
211 Park*

127

Baked Wahoo with Cream Crabmeat Sauce

4, 6-8 ounce fillets of
  Wahoo*
2 teaspoons onion,
  finely chopped
1/4 stick butter
1 pound cream cheese
2 cups fish stock*
1/4 cup white wine
1/4 teaspoon lemon
  juice
salt and pepper
1 cup lump crabmeat

* See glossary.

Sauté the onion in the butter. Add the cheese and the remaining ingredients except the crabmeat. Allow to simmer. Beat with a whisk until the sauce becomes smooth. Add the crabmeat. If necessary, adjust the consistency with any additional fish stock. Bake the fish 15-20 minutes at 350°. Remove to a plate and pour the sauce over the fish.
SERVES 4

Chef Mark Christian,
Aunt Chiladas

Beef Satay

Cut the sirloin into 1/4" slices, 2" long. Combine all of the marinade ingredients in a large mixing bowl. Place the meat in the marinade. Let stand overnight.

To prepare the peanut sauce, combine all of the ingredients in a saucepan over a moderate heat. Bring to a boil, then continue simmering until the sauce is thick. Adjust the seasonings, remove the bay leaf, and serve.

After the sirloin strips have marinated, skewer and cook on a griddle for about 1 to 1 1/2 minutes each side.

Serve with the peanut sauce and steamed rice on the side. Garnish with pieces of scallion (5" long) and half a cherry tomato.
SERVES 4

Chef Steve Felenczak,
Former Executive Chef,
Hyatt Regency

1 1/2 pounds sirloin tip

Marinade:
1/2 teaspoon curry powder
1 tablespoon lemon grass
2 tablespoons peanut oil
1/4 teaspoon garlic, chopped
1/4 teaspoon ginger, chopped
1 1/2 teaspoons chili garlic sauce
1 teaspoon soy sauce

Peanut Sauce:
1/4 cup raw peanuts or peanut butter
1/2 teaspoon garlic, minced
1/2 cup coconut milk
1/2 cup chicken stock*
1 teaspoon soy sauce
1 teaspoon sugar
1 teaspoon red pepper, ground
1 bay leaf
salt to taste

20, 4-ounce cod fillets

Beer Battered Cod Fillets with a Spicy Remoulade Sauce

Batter:
3 bottles beer
1 cup cream
1 cup water
12 eggs (yolks separate)
10 cups flour
1 tablespoon baking
   powder
1 tablespoon baking
   soda
1 teaspoon cayenne
   pepper
salt and pepper to taste
2 tablespoons Paul
   Prudomme seafood
   seasoning
12 egg whites (stiff)

Batter: Add liquid ingredients together, then separately add dry ingredients together. Pour dry into liquid, stirring well. Whip egg whites and fold into mix. Let stand 30 minutes.

(continued on next page)

(continued from previous page)

Remoulade sauce: Place all ingredients in bowl and mix well.

Dip fish into batter and fry to golden brown. Serve with remoulade.

SERVES 10

Remoulade Sauce:
3 cups mayonnaise
1/2 cup capers
1/2 cup red onion,
  small dice
1/2 cup relish
1/2 cup fine herbs
  (thyme, oregano,
  parsley)
  or herbs of your
  choice
2 tablespoons garlic
1/2 cup lemon juice
2 tablespoons blacken-
  ing seasoning
salt and pepper to taste

Chef Michael Wallace,
Hilton Resort

Broiled Grouper with Crab Imperial Sauce

4, 6-ounce grouper fillets
1/2 medium onion, diced
1/2 medium bell pepper, diced
2 teaspoons pimento, diced
1/2 cup butter
3 cups heavy cream
1 cup fish stock*
1/4 cup white wine
2 tablespoons lemon juice
salt and pepper
1 cup lump crabmeat
flour

* See glossary.

Sauté the onion, pepper, and pimento in a small amount of butter. When soft, add the cream, fish stock, wine, lemon juice, salt and pepper. Allow to simmer, then add the crabmeat. Thicken with a roux* mixture of blended butter and flour adding slowly until the desired consistency is reached. Broil the grouper and top with the sauce.
SERVES 4

*See glossary.

Chef Mark Christian,
Aunt Chiladas

Cajun Field Oysters in Gorgonzola Cream

Mix the flour and seasonings. Dredge the oysters in the mixture and pan sear. Remove from the pan. Sauté the shallots, add the cheese, wine and cream. Reduce until thickened. Salt and pepper to taste. Pour over the oysters. Garnish with wilted spinach.
SERVES 2

24 select oysters,
  shucked
1/2 cup flour
1 teaspoon cayenne
2 teaspoons paprika
2 teaspoons garlic,
  minced
1 teaspoon onion
  powder
1 teaspoon salt
1 teaspoon dried thyme
1 teaspoon white
  pepper

Sauce:
2 teaspoons shallots,
  chopped
Small amount of oil
1/4 cup gorgonzola
  cheese
1/2 cup white wine
1 cup heavy cream
salt and pepper to taste
24 ounces spinach

Chef Brad Blake,
Sunset Grille

Cajun Jambalaya

3/4 cup vegetable oil
1 cup all-purpose flour
1/2 cup celery, chopped
1 cup onions, chopped
1/2 cup green peppers,
  chopped
2 tablespoons garlic,
  minced
1/2 teaspoon cayenne
  pepper
1 tablespoon oregano
1 tablespoon basil
1, 16-ounce can
  chicken broth
1 pound chicken
  breast, cut into 1"
  cubes
1 cup kielbasa sausage,
  sliced
1/2 pound raw shrimp
  with tails still on
2 cups cooked rice

Heat 1/2 cup of the oil in a heavy skillet until very hot. Whisk in the flour, stirring constantly until smooth and dark. Reduce the heat by half and simmer for 20 minutes. Add the vegetables, garlic and spices, cooking for 5 minutes. In a large pot, heat the chicken broth. Add the vegetable mixture and simmer for 20 minutes.

Sauté the chicken and sausage for 5 minutes in the remaining 1/4 cup of oil. Pour off the oil, add to the flour mixture and then add the shrimp. Cook on medium high heat until the sauce is bubbling.

Serve over rice.

SERVES 4

Chef Johnny Highberger
Formerly of High Z's

134

Carolina Swamp Bog Chili

Combine the sausage and the ground chuck with the celery and onion and sauté. After 2 minutes, add the garlic. Combine all of the powdered seasonings, the bay leaves and the liquid smoke and add to the meat when cooked. Lightly precook the kidney beans and add to the meat mixture. Add the tomato paste and water to the meat mixture. Allow to simmer 3-5 hours.

YIELD: 1 GALLON

Chef Gary D. Williams,
The Sea Shack

1 pound ground chuck
1 pound Italian sausage
3-4 celery stalks, diced
1 small onion, diced
4 cloves of garlic, minced
1 tablespoon onion powder
2 tablespoons celery seed
1/4 cup salt
1 tablespoon white pepper
2 tablespoons cayenne pepper
1/4 cup Cajun seasoning
1/4 cup sugar
1/2 cup chili powder
2 tablespoons hickory flavored liquid smoke
3 bay leaves
1/2 pound red kidney beans
1, 6-ounce can tomato paste
1 1/2 cups water

Chicken Breast with Basil

1, 6-ounce skinless, boneless chicken breast
salt and pepper to taste
1/4 cup ricotta cheese
4 fresh basil leaves
1 egg yolk

Season the chicken breast with salt and pepper. Blend the cheese and add the finely chopped basil. Add the egg yolk and mix thoroughly. Stuff the cheese mixture into the chicken breast. Roll and secure with toothpicks. Bake in a 350° oven for 30 minutes or until done.
SERVES 1

Chef Gerard Thompson

Chicken Crêpes with Rosemary Cream Sauce

Preheat oven to 350°. Sauté the onion in most of the butter and add the chicken base or bouillon. Whisk in the cream and milk and add the herbs. Thicken the sauce on a low heat until bubbly around the edge. Sauté the chicken in the remaining butter until lightly browned. Cool slightly and cut into 1/4" strips.

Place 2 crêpes in each of six individual oblong casserole dishes. Place chicken strips (equivalent to 1 breast) on the crêpes. Add enough of the cream sauce to cover the strips. Roll the crêpes around the filling and top with more cream sauce. Add the cheese to cover the surface of the casseroles and brown in the oven close to the heat.
SERVES 6

1/2 cup onions, diced
1/2 pound butter
1/2 teaspoon chicken base or 1/2 cup chicken bouillon
1 pint whipping cream
1 pint milk
1 1/2 teaspoons rosemary
1/2 teaspoon thyme
6 boneless chicken breasts, skinned
12 crêpe shells
1/2 cup Swiss or Gruyère cheese, shredded

Chef Deborah Van Plew

137

Cincinnati Chili

5 pounds ground beef
2 large onions
1 small can tomato
  paste
5 cups chopped whole
  peeled tomatoes
5 tablespoons chili
  powder
1 tablespoon cinnamon
1 teaspoon cumin
1 teaspoon nutmeg
1 teaspoon ginger
2 quarts chicken stock*
1 cup brown sugar
salt and pepper
spaghetti, al denté**
sour cream
shredded cheddar

*May substitute canned
broth, bouillon or
water.
** See glossary

Brown ground beef in large pot, strain off grease. Add 1 onion finely diced to ground beef, continue cooking until onions are translucent. Add tomato paste to the pot, stirring, cook for 5 minutes. Add chopped tomatoes, bring to a boil. Add all spices, cook for 5 minutes. Add chicken stock and brown sugar. Let simmer for 1/2 hour, stirring occasionally. Salt and pepper to taste. Slice the 2nd onion into rings for garnish. Place spaghetti in a bowl, ladle on chili and top with onion rings, a dollop of sour cream and a sprinkle of shredded cheddar.

YIELD: ABOUT 1 GALLON

Chef Nick Anderson,
Just Pasta Café

Crab Cakes

Remove crust from bread and dice small. Add all dry ingredients to mixing bowl and toss. Fold in eggs and mayonnaise. Add Worcestershire and Tabasco. Mix gently. Portion into patties and sauté or deep fry.
SERVES 4

3/4 loaf white bread
2 pounds lump crab,
* picked for shells*
1 tablespoon parsley,
* chopped*
1 teaspoon Old Bay
* seasoning*
3 eggs
1 tablespoon
* mayonnaise*
1 1/4 tablespoons
* Worcestershire sauce*
Tabasco pepper sauce
* to taste*

Chef Michael Sigler,
Sigler's Rotisserie & Seafood

THE CHEFS OF HILTON HEAD

Crabcakes with Crawfish Hash

Crabcakes:
1 pound jumbo lump
  crabmeat
1 large egg, beaten
1/2 cup mayonnaise
3 tablespoons Dijon
  mustard
1 tablespoon
  Worcestershire
  sauce
2 cups packed fresh
  bread crumbs

Crawfish Hash:
3 tablespoons butter
1 pound cooked
  crawfish tail meat
2 large baking pota-
  toes, diced and boiled
  until tender, cooled
1 red pepper, diced
1 green pepper, diced
1 bunch green onions
salt and pepper to taste

Pick the shells out of the crab. Mix all of the remaining ingredients and add to the crab without breaking up the crab lumps. Form into 4-ounce patties. Brown on both sides and finish in a 400° oven for 10 minutes. Makes 8, 4-ounce patties.

To prepare the crawfish hash, melt the butter in a fry pan and sauté the remaining ingredients until the peppers are tender. Serve the crabcakes on top of the hash.

SERVES 4

Chef Jeff Ennis,
Formerly of the Boathouse II

140

Creole Stuffed Yellow Fin Tuna Steaks

Sauté the vegetables and alligator sausage in butter. Add the cornmeal and oyster essence. Fold all of the ingredients together. Stuff the tuna steaks with the mixture and grill. Baste with the barbecue sauce until the fish is done.
SERVES 4

1/2 onion, diced small
1 stalk celery, diced small
2 jalapeños, diced small
6 tablespoons jicama, diced small
1/4 cup alligator sausage, diced and cooked
1/4 stick butter
1 cup cornmeal
4 teaspoons oyster juice
4, 3" thick yellow fin tuna steaks
barbecue sauce of choice

Chef Richard Fausnacht,
Scott's Fish Market

Eggplant Parmigiano

4 eggplant slices
4 tablespoons oil
1/2 cup marinara
  sauce
4 tablespoons
  Parmesan, grated
1/2 cup mozzarella,
  shredded
1/2 cup ricotta cheese
parsley

Fry the eggplant in the oil until tender. Spoon 2 tablespoons of the marinara sauce onto the bottom of a baking dish. Add two slices of the eggplant. Add half of the Parmesan cheese, half of the mozzarella and all of the ricotta. Top with the remaining eggplant and cover with the marinara sauce. Add the remaining mozzarella and Parmesan cheese. Cook in a preheated 350° oven for 10 minutes. Garnish with two dots of marinara sauce and parsley.
SERVES 1

Chef Robert Montbleau,
Formerly of Port Royal Clubhouse

Fillet of Flounder with Tomatoes and Chervil

Clean the flounder and slice into four portions. Salt and pepper. Peel and dice the tomatoes and mix with the chervil and cheese. In a buttered dish, spread the shallots, then add the flounder and tomatoes. Bake for 7 minutes in a 450° oven. Mix the white wine and cream. Boil for 4 minutes. Adjust seasonings to taste. Place the flounder mixture on a plate, top with the sauce, and serve. SERVES 4

2, 8-ounce flounder fillets
4 tomatoes
1 bunch chervil*
10 tablespoons Swiss cheese, shredded
1/4 cup butter
2 shallots, finely diced
1 1/4 cups white wine
1 pint cream
salt and pepper to taste

* See glossary.

Chef Jean Loup Kunckler, Formerly of The Gaslight

Fresh Grouper with Leek-Mushroom Sauce

4 tablespoons olive oil
3 large leeks, chopped
1 pound mushrooms, sliced (Portobella or shiitake)
2 cloves garlic, chopped
1 1/2 cups dry white wine
2 cups whipping cream
1/4 cup parsley, chopped, plus garnish
salt and pepper
8, 6-ounce grouper fillets
all-purpose flour
4 tablespoons butter

Heat the olive oil in a heavy saucepan over medium heat. Add the leeks, mushrooms and garlic to the pan. Sauté until translucent, about 15 minutes. Add the wine and boil over high heat for about 5 minutes, until the liquid is reduced to 3 tablespoons. Add the cream and boil to sauce consistency. Stir in the parsley and season to taste with salt and pepper. Remove from the heat. Cover to keep warm.

Sprinkle the grouper fillets with salt and pepper. Dust lightly with flour. Melt the butter in a large nonstick skillet over medium-high heat. Add the grouper fillets to the skillet. Cook about 4 minutes per side. Transfer the cooked grouper to a serving platter. Spoon the sauce over the grouper and sprinkle with any additional parsley.
SERVES 8

Chef Mehdi Varedi,
Cattails

144

Fresh Scallops Provençal

Clean the scallops. Season with the salt and pepper and flour lightly. Heat the oil in a nonstick pan and cook the scallops until lightly brown. Remove from the pan and add garlic, parsley, tomatoes and thyme, cooking for 5 minutes. Add the butter and pour over the scallops. Serve with rice or boiled potatoes.

SERVES 4

1 1/2 pounds fresh scallops
salt, pepper, flour
2 tablespoons olive oil
3 cloves chopped garlic
1 1/2 tablespoons chopped parsley
2 medium tomatoes, diced
pinch of thyme
1 tablespoon soft butter

Chef Jean-Loup Kunckler,
Formerly of The Gaslight

145

Grilled Grouper over Pineapple Salsa

4, 6-ounce grouper
fillets

Salsa:
1 medium pineapple,
    cored, peeled and
    diced
1/2 small yellow pepper,
    diced
1/2 small red pepper,
    diced
1 small red onion, diced
2 cloves garlic, minced
1 jalapeño, diced
1 lime, zest and juice
1 lemon, zest and juice
6 tablespoons white
    wine
1/4 cup raspberry
    vinegar

Mix all of the ingredients other than the grouper. Marinate the fish in the mixture for 3 hours minimum, (overnight if possible.)

Grill the grouper on one side, about 4 minutes. Flip and continue grilling until done, about 2 - 3 minutes. Add the salsa to a pan and cook over medium heat until the liquid has evaporated. Plate the fish and serve with the salsa on top. SERVES 4

Chef Scott Sundermeyer,
Formerly of the Hyatt Regency

146

Grilled Salmon with a Peaches and Cream Sauce

For the sauce: Sauté peaches, deglaze with wine, brandy. Reduce. Add honey and orange juice and reduce down to a syrup. Add cream. Reduce 1/3. Mix with a hand mixer or blender and strain.

Grill salmon to desired doneness. Serve sauce over salmon.

SERVES 10

10, 8 ounce salmon fillets

Peaches and Cream Sauce:
2 cups peaches
1 cup rice wine
2 tablespoons brandy
2 tablespoons honey
1 cup orange juice
3/4 cup cream

Chef Michael Wallace,
Hilton Resort

Grilled Swordfish with Martini Butter

6, 7-ounce swordfish steaks, cut about 1" thick
1/3 cup olive oil
1/4 cup vermouth
1 1/2 teaspoons salt
1/2 teaspoon freshly ground pepper

Martini Butter:
2 tablespoons gin
1 tablespoon dry vermouth
1/3 cup pimiento-stuffed green olives (about 12 medium)
8 tablespoons unsalted butter, at room temperature
1/2 teaspoon grated fresh lemon zest
dash of cayenne

Brush the fish on both sides with the olive oil and vermouth. Season with the salt and pepper. Cover with plastic wrap and marinate 30 minutes at room temperature. Prepare a hot grill fire. Oil the grids and set 4" to 6" from coals or gas flame. Grill the swordfish, turning once and moving as necessary to make nice grid marks and to prevent scorching, until the fish is just opaque in the center, about 10 - 12 minutes total. Serve with a dollop of martini butter on top of each piece of swordfish. The heat of the fish will melt the butter into a sumptuous "white loudmouth" sauce.

To prepare the martini butter, boil the gin and vermouth over a high heat in a small non-reactive saucepan until the liquid is reduced to 1 tablespoon, (2 to 4 minutes.) Remove from the heat and let cool.

In a food processor, combine the reduced mixture, with the olives, butter, lemon zest, and cayenne. Process until the olives are minced and the mixture is well blended. Martini butter can be stored several days in the refrigerator, or for weeks in the freezer.
SERVES 6

Dotti Trivison, Food Editor
The Island Packet

148

Grilled Tuna with Pineapple Chutney

6, 1" thick tuna steaks
1 pineapple, peeled
  and cored
1 medium onion
1 red pepper
3 tablespoons olive oil
1 tablespoon flour
pinch of allspice*
1/4 cup apple juice
pinch of cumin
pinch of cayenne
1/4 cup honey

* See glossary.

To prepare the chutney, cut the pineapple, onion and red pepper into 1/4" pieces. Heat the oil in a medium pan on high. Add the onion and sauté until tender. Add the flour and stir. Stir in the red pepper, pineapple and allspice. Add the apple juice, cumin, cayenne and honey. Bring to a boil. Cover and reduce to low. Cook for 1 hour, stirring occasionally. Remove from the heat. May be served chilled or warm.

To prepare the tuna, brush the tuna steaks with olive oil and grill 4 minutes on each side. Remove to a platter, cover with chutney and serve. SERVES 6

Chef Richard Canestrari,
211 Park

1 pork tenderloin
2 tablespoons jerk
  spice*
2 tablespoons olive oil

Sweet and Sour Sauce:
1/2 onion, diced
1 tablespoon garlic,
  chopped
2 tablespoons ginger,
  chopped
2 tablespoons oil
2 tablespoons brown
  sugar
2 tablespoons red wine
  vinegar
1/3 cup ketchup
2 tablespoons chicken
  stock

2 tablespoons pesto
  (store bought is fine)
1 tablespoon crumbled
  feta cheese

*See glossary.

Island Spiced Pork Tenderloin with Pesto, Sweet and Sour and Feta Cheese

Trim the pork tenderloin and marinate it in jerk spice and olive oil for 1 hour.

To prepare the sweet and sour sauce, sauté the onion, garlic, and ginger in the oil for 5 minutes. Add the brown sugar and dissolve. Add the vinegar, ketchup and stock. Simmer for 20 minutes. Cool and set aside.

Grill the pork to the desired temperature. Slice and place around your favorite starch. Top with the cooled sweet and sour sauce, pesto and crumbled feta cheese.

SERVES 4

Chef Keith Tanenbaum,
Alligator Grille

150

Kentucky Bourbon Marinated Ribeye Steaks

Combine first 8 ingredients in the bowl of a food processor. Pulse. Add the oil in a stream while the machine is running. Combine until emulsified.

Put the steaks in a shallow dish and cover with the marinade. Allow to marinate at least 8 hours, or overnight. Grill the steaks and serve with thinly sliced french-fried onion rings.
SERVES 4

1/4 cup apple cider vinegar
1/4 cup Maker's Mark Bourbon
3 tablespoons soy sauce
2 cloves garlic
1/2" piece of ginger, peeled
2 tablespoons brown sugar
1/4 cup chili sauce
1/2 teaspoon salt
2 cups salad oil
4, 1"-thick ribeye steaks

Chef Melissa Cochran,
Julep's

Lamb Chops
à la Landon

2, 8-ounce, 3/4" thick
lamb chops
2 cloves garlic, minced
1 teaspoon black
pepper
1 teaspoon seasoned
salt
pinch of thyme
1/2 stick margarine
1 teaspoon onion
powder
1/4 pound melted
butter
2 tablespoons sherry
mint jelly

Rub the chops until well coated with garlic, pepper, seasoned salt, thyme, margarine and onion powder. Melt the butter in a skillet. When hot, sear the chops until dark on one side. Turn, cover, and reduce the heat. Cook until desired doneness.

Deglaze* the pan with the sherry and serve the chops with pan juices and mint jelly. Serve with parsleyed red skin potatoes and asparagus with hollandaise.

SERVES 2

* See glossary.

*Chef Brad Terhune,
Captain's Seafood*

Marinated Grilled Tuna Loin over Wilted Arugula

4, 8-ounce tuna loin
steaks
1 cup vinaigrette
dressing
1 cup fried corn
tortilla strips
2 cups fresh arugula
1/2 cup sesame oil
1/4 cup rice wine
vinegar
1/2 cup red, green and
yellow peppers, finely
diced
2 tablespoons Dijon
mustard
salt and pepper to taste

Marinate the tuna loin steaks in your favorite vinaigrette dressing overnight. Cut the corn tortillas into thin strips and fry until crispy. Set aside.

Wash and stem the fresh arugula. Combine the sesame oil, rice wine vinegar, diced peppers, Dijon mustard and salt and pepper. Mix well. Grill the tuna loin medium-rare, to medium. Place the arugula on a plate. Set the grilled tuna over the arugula. Top with the sesame vinaigrette and sprinkle the corn tortilla strips on top. Serve warm.

SERVES 4

Chef Michael Diehl,
Anna's Beachside Café

Marinated Mahi Mahi

3 cups apple cider
6 tablespoons soy sauce
1/4 pound unsalted
   butter
1 tablespoon garlic,
   minced
4 Mahi fillets, 8-10
   ounces each

Bring the cider, soy sauce, butter and garlic to a boil. Reduce by half. Cool to room temperature. Marinate the Mahi fillets for at least 12 hours in the cider mixture. Grill over charcoal.

SERVES 4

Chef Johnny Highberger
Formerly of High Z's

Marinated Oven-Roasted Tenderloin

Place the tenderloin, onion, garlic and herbs in a large pan. Pour the wine and 1 cup of the oil over the meat and season. Marinate for 6 hours.

Sear the tenderloin in a large saucepan with 2 tablespoons of oil until browned all over. Roast for 15 - 18 minutes in a preheated 400° oven until medium rare. Remove to a warm plate and set aside.

To prepare the coulis, seed and coarsely chop each color pepper and place in separate pans. To each, add 1 chopped onion, 3 cups water, 3 tablespoons oil and season to taste. Boil until softened. Purée each separately in a food processor until smooth. Strain and season. Pour the coulis on the plate in red and yellow stripes. Slice the tenderloin and place around the sauce. SERVES 8 - 10

Tenderloin:
2 to 3 pound center-cut tenderloin
1 large onion, chopped
1 large clove garlic, chopped
2 sprigs rosemary, chopped
2 sprigs thyme, chopped
1 cup red wine
1 cup plus 2 table-spoons peanut oil
season to taste

Coulis:*
6 red bell peppers
6 golden bell peppers
2 large onions
6 cups water
6 tablespoons oil
season to taste

* See glossary.

Chef Jim McLain,
Callawassie Island

1 1/2 pounds fresh
Norwegian salmon
2 tablespoons lemon
and lime juice
salt
1 tablespoon freshly
ground pepper
1 tablespoon crushed
coriander seeds
2 tablespoons chopped
basil
2 tablespoons extra-
virgin olive oil

Marinated Salmon in Basil and Olive Oil

Peel and skin the salmon. Refrigerate for 2 hours. Chill 4 plates.

Using a very sharp knife, thinly slice the salmon without breaking the meat. Brush the bottom of the plates with lemon/lime juice. Place the salmon on the plates and brush the fish very lightly with more juice. Season with the salt, pepper, coriander and basil. Then brush the salmon with olive oil. Chill for 2 hours. Serve with French white toast and a glass of Chardonnay. SERVES 4

*Chef Jean-Loup Kunckler,
Formerly of The Gaslight*

Marinated Swordfish with Cilantro Lime Butter

1/2 pound butter

3/4 cup fresh cilantro, chopped

1 tablespoon cracked black pepper

1 teaspoon salt

juice of 4 limes

2 cups soy sauce

1/4 cup olive oil

3 cloves garlic, minced

1/4 cup fresh ginger, minced

2 tablespoons red pepper, crushed

1/4 cup honey

4, 7-ounce swordfish or tuna steaks

Let the butter come to room temperature. In a mixing bowl, whip butter until fluffy. Add 1/4 cup cilantro, pepper, salt and lime juice and mix. Place the butter mixture on a sheet of plastic wrap and roll into an even cylinder, using the wrap to shape. Chill.

Mix the soy sauce, oil, remaining cilantro, garlic, ginger, red pepper and honey. Marinate the steaks for 24 hours.

Grill the steaks over medium heat 4-5 minutes per side, or until it is firm to the touch. Top each steak with a 1/2" slice of cilantro-lime butter. SERVES 4

Chef Sonny Tanksley,
Formerly of Sigler's Rotisserie

1 1/4 cups macaroni
1 cup plain, non-fat
  yogurt
1/2 cup feta cheese,
  crumbled
2 cloves garlic, minced
1 tablespoon fresh dill,
  chopped
1/2 teaspoon black
  pepper
1/2 pound 16-20 count
  shrimp
6 ounces sea scallops
8-10 ounces fresh
  spinach
salt to taste

Mediterranean Shrimp, Scallop, and Spinach Macaroni

Prepare the pasta according to the package. Stir together the yogurt, feta cheese, garlic, dill, and pepper in a large mixing bowl. Two minutes before the pasta is done, stir the shrimp, scallops, and spinach into the pot with the pasta. Drain the seafood, spinach, and pasta thoroughly. Stir in the yogurt, feta cheese mixture and season to taste with salt. Serve immediately.

SERVES 4

Chef Anthony Scott,
Scott's Fish Market

Mustard Grilled Chicken with Fresh Herbs

Mix all of the marinade ingredients together. Cover the chicken breasts with the marinade and refrigerate about 24 - 36 hours.

Grill the chicken breasts over a medium fire until just done and the juices run clear. Do not overcook.

Can be served alone, or on a bed of flavored pasta such as a lemon-basil linguini or tarragon fettucccine.

SERVES 6

Chef Steve Hancotte,
Stripes

Marinade:
2 1/2 cups Dijon
   mustard
1 cup dry white wine
2 tablespoons fresh
   basil, chopped
2 tablespoons fresh
   tarragon, chopped
2 tablespoons fresh
   hives, chopped
1 tablespoon fresh dill,
   chopped
1 teaspoon fresh thyme,
   chopped
2 teaspoons seasoned
   salt
2 teaspoons cracked
   black pepper
1 medium onion,
   minced

6, chicken breasts,
   halved with skin and
   bones

Norwegian Salmon in Champagne Fennel Sauce

1, 7-ounce salmon
fillet
flour seasoned with
salt and pepper
1/4 cup oil
1/4 cup champagne
2 tablespoons ver-
mouth
1 teaspoon shallots,
chopped
1 teaspoon fennel,
finely chopped
1 tablespoon lemon
juice
2 tablespoons heavy
cream
1 tablespoon butter
1/2 cup linguini,
cooked

Dredge the salmon in the seasoned flour and sauté in heated oil. Drain the oil into another pan for the sauce. Place the salmon in a 200° oven to keep warm. Start the sauce by adding the wine and vermouth to the oil. Add the shallots, fennel and juice. Add the cream and butter, stirring constantly. Return the salmon to the sauce and serve over linguini.

SERVES 1

Chef Robert Montbleau,
Formerly of Port Royal Clubhouse

Osso Buco with Autumn Root Vegetables

Heat the oil in a pan. Dust the shanks in flour and brown in the pan. Remove and keep warm. Add the onions, garlic and sauté. Add the white wine, tomatoes and tomato paste. Simmer for 15 minutes. Add the chicken stock, thyme, salt and pepper, veal shanks and diced root vegetables. Cover and simmer for 1 hour, or until fork tender. Remove the shanks to a bowl and skim the fat from the sauce. Spoon the vegetables around the shank and spoon the sauce on top of the shank. Serve hot. SERVES 4

1/3 cup olive oil
4, 1" veal shank pieces, with bone
1/3 cup flour
1 medium onion, diced
3 cloves garlic, minced
1 cup white wine
1/4 cup tomato paste
2 cups chicken stock*
fresh thyme to taste
salt and pepper to taste
1/2 cup each diced carrots, turnips, rutabagas
2 cups seeded, diced tomatoes

*See glossary.

Chef Michael Diehl,
Anna's Beachside Café

Oven Steamed Salmon and Scallop Terrine

2 pounds fresh
Norwegian salmon
1 1/2 pounds fresh sea
scallops
juice of 1 lemon
2 tablespoons soy sauce
1/2 teaspoon Tabasco
pepper sauce
4 tablespoons parsley,
chopped
6 eggs
1/2 cup heavy cream

Sauce:
2 tablespoons fresh dill,
chopped
3 roasted yellow bell
peppers, peeled and
seeded
3 cups white wine
1 cup herb butter,
softened
salt and pepper to taste

Preheat the oven to 400°. Fillet the salmon, removing the skin and bones. Remove the muscles from the scallops. Put the scallops in a food processor and add the lemon juice, soy sauce, Tabasco, parsley, eggs and process. Slowly add the cream until blended. Season with salt and pepper.

Slice salmon thinly. Grease a terrine* with butter. Alternate layers of salmon and scallop mousse until full. Cover with waxed paper and bake for 25 - 30 minutes. Remove and set aside.

To prepare the sauce, cut the bell peppers into diamond shapes. Combine with the wine and the dill in a sauté pan and reduce by half. Add the butter, and reduce until creamy. Season with salt and pepper.

Serve slices of the terrine with the warm sauce on top.
SERVES 6 - 8

* See glossary.

*Chef Jim McLain,
Callawassie Island*

162

Oyster Pie

Sauté oysters, shallots, celery and cajun spice for 2 minutes. Add cream and reduce by half. Finish with sherry. Mix saltines, cheddar, scallions and butter in bowl. Place oysters in shallow bowl and top with saltines mixture. Brown 4 minutes in oven at 450°.

SERVES 4

1/2 tablespoon butter
24 shucked oysters
1 tablespoon chopped shallots
1 tablespoon chopped celery
1/4 teaspoon cajun spice
1 1/2 cups heavy cream
1/2 tablespoon sherry
1/2 cup crushed saltines
1/4 cup grated cheddar
2 tablespoons melted butter
1 tablespoon chopped scallions

Chef John Briody,
Colleton River Plantation

Palmetto Penne

Pesto:

3 red bell peppers,
 roasted, peeled,
 stemmed, & seeded
3 cloves garlic, minced
1 cup olive oil
1/2 cup Parmesan
 cheese, grated
1/2 cup fresh parsley,
 de-stemmed and
 packed tightly
1/2 cup toasted pecans

4, 6-ounce skinless chicken
 breasts
1 tablespoon olive oil
2 large portobella
 mushrooms
1 small can quartered
 artichokes
4 cups cooked penne pasta
1/2 cup white wine
1 cup packed fresh,
 de-stemmed spinach
 leaves
4 stalks sliced hearts of
 palm
4 tablespoons toasted
 pine nuts

Place all of the ingredients for the pesto into a food processor fitted with a metal blade. Pulse the machine until the ingredients are thoroughly puréed. Set aside.

Grill the chicken breasts and cut into 1" cubes. Set aside. De-stem and cut the portobella mushrooms into 1/2" cubes and set aside.

Pour the olive oil into a large sauté pan over medium-high heat. Add the mushrooms and artichoke hearts. Sauté them for 1 minute, then add 1 1/2 cups of the pesto sauce, chicken, penne and white wine. Toss this mixture until the wine has reduced, about 5 minutes. Next, add the spinach, and toss again. Season to taste with salt and pepper and serve in large pasta bowls garnished with the hearts of palm and pine nuts.
SERVES 4

Chef Jon C. Gilliam,
Executive Chef, Café Europa

164

Pan Fried Quail with Wild Mushrooms and Vine Ripe Tomatoes

Heat a skillet and add the olive oil. Dust the quail in the cornmeal and brown in the oil. Remove and keep warm.

Add the onions, garlic, and mushrooms to the pan and sauté. Add the wine, cilantro, tomatoes, and salt and pepper. Simmer for 10 minutes and add the quail. Cover and simmer for 20 more minutes. Remove the quail to a plate. Reduce the sauce by 1/3 and spoon over the quail. Top with the spring onions.

SERVES 4

1/4 cup olive oil
4 boneless quail (6 ounces each)
1/2 cup yellow corn meal
1/2 cup onion, diced
4 garlic cloves (thinly sliced)
1/2 cup shiitaki * mushrooms, sliced
1/2 cup portobella mushrooms, sliced
1/3 cup Merlot wine
1/4 cup cilantro, diced
3 medium vine-ripe tomatoes (peeled and seeded)
salt and pepper to taste
4 spring onions lightly grilled

* See glossary.

Chef Michael Diehl,
Anna's Beachside Café

1 tablespoon shallots
2 tablespoons pro-
   sciutto ham, finely
   diced
2 tablespoons olive oil
2 tablespoons butter
1 teaspoon garlic,
   chopped
1/4 cup zucchini,
   halved and sliced
1/4 cup heavy cream
pinch of basil
pinch of parsley
2 tablespoons
   Parmesan cheese,
   grated
2 tablespoons Romano
   cheese, grated
salt and pepper

Pasta with Zucchini and Prosciutto

Sauté the shallots and prosciutto in the oil and butter. Add the garlic and zucchini. Add the cream, basil, parsley and cheeses to thicken. Season with the salt and pepper and serve over fettuccine. SERVES 1

Chef Robert Montbleau,
Formerly of Port Royal Clubhouse

Pecan-Crusted Salmon

1 cup pecans, chopped
1/4 cup brown sugar
1/2 cup all-purpose
  flour
2 teaspoons salt
2 teaspoons white
  pepper
4, 6-8 ounce skinless
  salmon fillets
milk
vegetable oil
1 stick butter

In a food processor, slowly combine the pecans, brown sugar, flour, salt and pepper. If the machine begins to clog, use smaller amounts of each ingredient and make several batches. Set aside 1/2 cup of the mixture.

Soak the salmon fillets in milk for 10 minutes prior to preparation. Heat 1/4 inch of oil in a large heavy skillet. Press the salmon into the pecan mixture until coated. Carefully cook until well browned on all sides. Do not turn your back on this step even for a second. Brown sugar will burn! Remove the salmon and place onto a cooking pan into a preheated 400° oven for 10 minutes. In a small saucepan, melt the butter and add the remaining pecan mixture. Place the cooked fish on a plate and top with the butter. This dish will stand up well with a Chardonnay or Merlot. SERVES 4

Chef David R. Hawkes,
Corner Market Café

Penne in Cream Sauce with Sausage

1 tablespoon butter
1 tablespoon olive oil
1 medium onion, thinly sliced
3 garlic cloves, minced
1 pound sweet Italian sausage, casings removed
2/3 cup dry white wine
1 14 1/2-ounce can diced, peeled tomatoes with their juices
1 cup whipping cream
6 tablespoons Italian parsley, chopped
salt and pepper
1 pound penne pasta
1 cup freshly-grated Parmesan cheese

Melt the butter and oil in a heavy large skillet over medium-high heat. Add the onion and garlic and sauté until golden brown. Add the sausage and sauté until golden brown and cooked through, breaking up with the back of a spoon. Drain excess drippings from the skillet. Add the wine to skillet and boil until almost all liquid evaporates. Add the tomatoes with their juices; simmer 3 minutes. Add the cream and simmer until sauce thickens slightly, about 5 minutes. Stir in 4 tablespoons of parsley. Season to taste with salt and pepper. Remove from the heat. (Sauce can be prepared 1 day ahead. Cover and refrigerate.)

Cook the pasta in a large pot of boiling, salted water until tender but still firm to the bite. Drain the pasta. Transfer to a large bowl.

Bring the sauce to a simmer. Pour the sauce over the pasta. Add 3/4 cup of the cheese and toss to coat. Sprinkle with the remaining 1/4 cup of the cheese and 2 tablespoons of parsley.
SERVES 4

Chef "Neno" Giovani,
Neno Il Toscano

Penne Puttanesca

Cook paste aldenté. In a separate pan, heat oil and garlic. Add anchovies and cook till fully dissolved. Once dissolved, add olives. After the olives juice has been extracted, add tomatoes. Season. Cover and simmer for 6 minutes. Add 1/2 basil and capers. Adjust seasoning. Simmer until tomatoes appear orange in color. Toss with pasta. Garnish with remaining basil.
SERVES 1

4 - 5 ounces penne pasta
1 ounce olive oil
1 clove garlic
2 anchovy fillets
6 pitted black olives (Gaeta or Kalamata)
9 ounces tomatoes peeled and diced
salt and pepper to taste
3 basil leaves, chopped
12 capers

Francesco Scotto,
Trattoria la Spiaggia

Poached Grouper with Spiced Seed Crust

1 English cucumber,
fine julienne*

3 tablespoons kosher
salt

1/4 cup jicama,*
julienned

2 tablespoons dill,
chopped

3 tablespoon chives,
chopped

1/8 cup sherry vinegar

2 tablespoons olive
oil

white pepper

2 large parsnip
roots, peeled and
coarsely
shredded

2 baking potatoes,
peeled and coarsely
chopped

1 small white onion,
peeled and finely
chopped

salt

1 lime, juiced

1/4 cup low-fat sour
cream

1 cup dry white wine

In a medium bowl, combine the cucumbers and kosher salt and mix until well combined. Let set for about 10 minutes or until the cucumbers have released their moisture. Rinse under cold water and pat dry. Return the cucumbers to a medium bowl, add the jicama, dill, 1 tablespoon chives, sherry vinegar and olive oil. Mix until well combined. Adjust the seasoning with white pepper. Set aside.

In a medium pot, combine the parsnip root, potatoes, onion, and a generous pinch of salt. Fill the pot with cold water to cover and bring to a simmer over medium heat. Cook until tender, about 20 - 30 minutes. Drain well and return to the same pot. Add the lime juice and sour cream. With a mixer attachment, mix until well combined. Adjust the seasoning to taste with salt and pepper. Keep warm.

In a small saucepan, combine the wine, water, bay leaf, salt and parsley stems. Bring to a boil

(continued on next page)

170

(continued from previous page) over a high heat and simmer for about 5 minutes. Meanwhile, in a medium saucepan, over high heat, combine the sesame seed, poppyseed, celery seed and dill. Heat until lightly toasted and aromatic, about 1 - 2 minutes. Pour the olive oil in a glass baking dish, large enough to hold the four fish fillets, without overlapping. Toss the fillets until well coated with oil. Season with salt and black pepper. Generously sprinkle the seed mixture on top of the fish fillets to form a crust. Gently pour the wine mixture around the fish. Cover the baking dish with foil and simmer over a medium heat until the fish is cooked through, about 8 - 10 minutes. Carefully remove the fish from the liquid onto a draining platter. To serve, make a bed of parsnip purée in the center of four serving plates. Arrange the cucumber salad around the purée and place a fillet atop the purée. Spoon the vinaigrette around the fish. Sprinkle the radishes and remaining chives on top.
SERVES 4

Chef Keith Josefiak,
Starfire Contemporary Bistro

1 cup water
1 bay leaf
parsley stems, reserved
* from chopped parsley*
pinch of salt
2 tablespoons white
* sesame seeds*
2 tablespoons
* poppyseeds*
1 tablespoon celery
* seeds*
1 tablespoon dried dill
2 tablespoons olive oil
4 portions of grouper
* or halibut, 6-ounces*
* each, trimmed of*
* skin and fat*
salt to taste
black pepper to taste
1 recipe Scallion
* Vinaigrette*
* (See under Salad*
* Dressings)*
6 radishes, julienned
2 tablespoons chives,
chopped

*See glossary.

Quail with Mustard Sauce

8 semi-boneless quail
1 cup all-purpose flour
1/4 cup butter
1/3 cup brandy
3/4 cup chicken stock, *
  or chicken broth
1 tablespoon Dijon
  mustard
1/2 teaspoon lemon
  juice
1 teaspoon
  Worcestershire sauce
1/4 teaspoon pepper

* may substitute
canned broth, bouil-
lon, or water.

Dredge the quail in flour and sauté in butter. Brown both sides and remove from the pan.

Deglaze the pan with the brandy and add the remaining ingredients. Add the quail and cover. Simmer for 10-15 minutes.
SERVES 4

Chef Jeff Hendrickson

Quesadilla of Balsamic-ginger Barbecued Duck with Peppers and Mango

3 tablespoons clarified
  butter *
1 small yellow onion,
  minced
2 cloves of garlic,
  minced
1/4 cup balsamic
  vinegar
2 tablespoons brown
  sugar
1 tablespoon fresh
  ginger, minced
1 teaspoon cinnamon
1 teaspoon salt
white pepper to taste
12 ounces cooked,
  shredded duck,
  reserved warm
2 poblano peppers
2 red bell peppers
2 small packages of
  goat cheese
1 mango, skinned and
  sliced
8, 6" flour tortillas

Sauté the onion and garlic in the clarified butter until softened. Add the remaining ingredients (vinegar, sugar, ginger, cinnamon, salt & pepper) to the pan, bring to a boil, then reduce the heat and simmer until the sauce thickens (about three minutes). Toss the duck with the sauce in the pan, remove from heat and reserve (warm). Roast the poblano and bell peppers, remove the skins and cut into thin strips. Spread sinful amounts of goat cheese on each tortilla. Add a generous layer of duck, mango, poblano and red pepper to four of the tortillas and cover with the remaining four to make four quesadillas. Warm each quesadilla in a pan over medium heat until golden brown and crispy. Serve and enjoy!
SERVES 4

Chef Michael Ramey,
Tavern on the Creek

* See Glossary.

Rabbit Sautéed with Dijon Mustard

1, 3-pound rabbit, in
  6 pieces*
salt and pepper
1/2 cup Dijon mustard
5 tablespoons butter
1/4 pound salt pork
1 cup pearl
  onions
3 cloves garlic,
  peeled
bouquet garni of
  thyme, bayleaf, and
  parsley**
1 cup white wine
6 large mushrooms,
  quartered
1/4 cup heavy cream
1 tablespoon lemon
  juice

*Roasting chicken or
capon may be
substituted.

**See glossary.

Rinse the rabbit meat under water, then salt and pepper and coat with mustard. Heat the butter in a high-sided frying pan until it foams, adding the rabbit, pork, onions, garlic and bouquet garni. Cook on medium-high heat for 20 minutes, turning often. Add the wine, scraping often to keep from sticking. Add the mushrooms. Cook over moderate heat for 15 minutes. Lower the heat, cover and simmer for 10 minutes. Remove the meat and onions to a hot platter. Whisk in the heavy cream. If all the wine has evaporated, add a 1/2 cup of water. Heat almost to boiling. Whisk in the lemon juice. Correct spices to taste. Spoon over the rabbit.
SERVES 4

Chef Dave Plemmons

Red Snapper Casino

To prepare the Casino butter, soften the butter and mix with all of the ingredients. Roll into a 1 1/2" diameter log and wrap in plastic. Refrigerate until needed.

To prepare the red snapper, dredge the snapper in the flour. Heat a sauté pan and sauté the snapper in the oil, skin side up. In a separate pan, melt the Casino butter. Add the remaining ingredients, except the julienned vegetables.

Cover the bottom of a plate with the julienned vegetables and top them with the fish, clams and Casino Butter.

SERVES 1

Chef Michael Sigler,
Sigler's Rotisserie & Seafood

Casino Butter:
1 pound unsalted
* butter*
1/4 cup shallots, diced
1 cup green peppers,
* diced*
1 cup red peppers,
* diced*
1 tablespoon Tabasco
* pepper sauce*
1/2 cup white wine.
7 ounces red snapper
* fillet*
2 tablespoons flour
1/4 cup butter
oil
4 small clams
1 tablespoon chopped
* raw bacon*
1 tablespoon parsley,
* chopped*
1 tablespoon white wine
1/2 lemon
2 tablespoons julienne*
* of mixed vegetables, such*
* as carrots, zucchini,*
* yellow squash, etc.*

*See glossary

175

Roasted Quail Stuffed with Andouille Sausage and Greens

1 pound andouille
  sausage or chorizo
1 pound kielbasa or
  smoked sausage
2 tablespoons butter
2, 8-ounce boxes of
  chopped frozen
  collards or 2 cups
  cooked fresh collards,
  chopped
8 quail, rib cages
  removed
salt and pepper

Cut the sausages into 1" pieces and grind in a food processor. Place the butter in a saucepan. Add the sausage. Cook the sausage to heat through, adding the packages of chopped collards. Mix together. Cool the stuffing. Season the quail with salt and pepper inside and out. Stuff the cavities with the collard/sausage mixture. Place the quail in a roasting pan. In a 425° oven, roast for 15 minutes until nicely browned and stuffing is hot inside. Serve 2 birds per person with mashed sweet potatoes.
SERVES 4

*Chef Melissa Cochran,
Julep's*

Roasted Lamb Dijonnaise

Clean and trim lamb rack. Bake in oven 10minutes at 350 degrees. For bread crumb mixture, blend bread crumbs with minced garlic and fresh chopped herbs, add oil to moisten. Remove lamb rack from oven and coat with Dijon mustard, then cover with breadcrumb mixture. Return to oven and bake an additional 10-15 minutes.
SERVES 2-4

1 Lamb Rack
 (New Zealand)
Dijon Mustard

Bread Crumb Mixture:
8 ounces Italian bread
 crumbs
1 ounce garlic, minced
1 teaspoon each (fresh)
 chopped basil, thyme
 & oregano
olive oil

Sous-Chef Avery Early,
Okatie Creek Clubhouse
Sun City Hilton Head

Salmon Southern Style

4 cups chicken stock*
1/4 cup heavy cream
1 1/2 cups stone-
 ground white grits
6 sprigs fresh dill
salt and pepper to taste
1/2 stick butter at
 room temperature
1 tablespoon white
 wine
1 teaspoon shallots,
 chopped
4, 8-ounce salmon
 fillets

* may substitute
canned broth, bouil-
lon, or water.

In a saucepan, combine the chicken stock and cream, and bring to a boil. Stir in the grits, stirring often to prevent from sticking. Turn heat to low and simmer the grits until thick and bubbly, approximately 25 minutes. Chop 3 sprigs of the dill and stir into the grits. Add salt and pepper and set aside.

Next, whip the butter until soft and airy, adding the remaining dill (finely chopped), white wine, shallots and salt and pepper to taste. Using a pastry bag, form the butter into 1 1/2 ounce rosettes* and chill. Season and grill the salmon fillets. Spoon 1-cup dollops of the grits onto plates, topping them with the grilled salmon and a butter rosette.
SERVES 4

* See glossary.

Executive Chef Jon C. Gilliam,
Café Europa

178

Saltimbocca di Vitelli

Dust veal chop with flour. Braise both sides in olive oil. Add mushrooms, and Marsala - burn off alcohol. Top off chop with proscuitto, sage and mozzarella. Cover, bake 400° until desired doneness. Remove from oven. Plate chop. Add butter to pan, reduce sauce while stirring constantly. Pour over chop.
SERVES 1

1 frenched veal chop
1 tablespoon flour for dusting
1 ounce extra virgin olive oil
3 ounces quartered button mushrooms
3 ounces Marsala wine
1 slice prosciutto di parma
3-4 sage leaves
1 slice fresh mozzarella
1 tablespoon butter

Chef Francesco Scotto,
Trattoria la Spiaggia

Sautéed Shrimp and Scallops with a Parmesan, Tasso Ham Cream Sauce

10 medium shrimp,
  peeled
18 sea scallops
2 tablespoons olive oil
1/4 pound tasso ham,*
  cut into thin strips
1/2 tablespoon shallots
1/2 teaspoon garlic
1 tablespoon fresh
  thyme
1 teaspoon basil
1/2 teaspoon dill,
  minced
1/4 cup dry sherry
2 tablespoons lemon
  juice
1 1/2 cups heavy cream
4 tablespoons
  Parmesan cheese
1 pound fresh angel
  hair pasta, cooked
salt and pepper to taste

* See glossary.

Sauté the shrimp and scallops in the olive oil on low heat. Add the tasso ham, shallots, garlic and herbs. Increase the heat to medium-high. Add the sherry, lemon juice, and heavy cream. Bring to a boil, then reduce the heat. Fold in the cheese. Place the pasta in a serving bowl and pour the sauce over the top.
SERVES 2

Chef Dallas Pierce III
Formerly of Harbourmasters

180

Sautéed Veal, Prosciutto and Portobella Mushroom with Rigatoni

In a large, heavy skillet, heat 1/4" of vegetable oil. Thinly pound the veal and dredge lightly in flour. Sauté on both sides, reducing the heat to avoid scorching. Remove the veal and drain off the oil. Carefully deglaze the pan with the wine and return to the heat. Add the ham, mushroom and pine nuts and stir until the ingredients begin to cook. Add the stock and seasonings and stir for several minutes until the mixture is thoroughly heated. Add the cheese and cream and reduce until thickened. Cut the veal into strips and introduce back to the skillet. Salt and pepper to taste. Add the rigatoni and toss until coated. Serve immediately. This dish does well with a Sauvignon Blanc or a lighter red such as a Chianti or Côtes-du-Rhône.

SERVES 4

*Chef David R. Hawkes,
Corner Market Café*

vegetable oil
1 pound veal cutlet
1/2 cup all-purpose flour
1/4 cup dry white wine
3/4 cup prosciutto ham, julienned
1 large portobella mushroom cap, chopped
1/4 cup roasted pine nuts
1/4 - 1/2 cup chicken stock*
1 tablespoon garlic, chopped
salt
white pepper
1/4 cup Parmesan cheese, grated
1 cup heavy whipping cream
4 cups cooked rigatoni

* See glossary.

Scalloped Pork Chops with Oyster Dressing

1 stick butter
1 cup onion, diced
1 cup red bell peppers,
    diced
1 cup celery, diced
1 cup water
1/2 pint oysters with
    liquid
3 1/2 cups crackers,
    crushed
salt and pepper
Worcestershire sauce
4, 1/2" thick pork
    chops
1 clove garlic, minced
onion powder
2 tablespoons butter
2 cups hot milk

To prepare the dressing, melt the butter and add the onion, red pepper and celery. Cook for 1 minute on medium-high heat. Add the water and oysters with liquid and heat to a boil. Add the crackers. Season with salt, pepper and Worcestershire sauce.

Sprinkle the pork chops liberally with the pepper, salt, garlic and onion powder on both sides. Place them in a baking dish and cover them with the oyster dressing. Fill the dish with the hot milk just to the top of the oyster dressing and bake, covered, for 1 hour, 15 minutes in a 350° oven. SERVES 4

Chef Brad Terhune,
Captain's Seafood

182

Seafood Crêpes

Sauté the carrots and celery in the butter. Add the next eight ingredients and whisk over low heat until bubbly and thickened. Put your favorite cooked seafood in crêpes and follow directions for the chicken crepes on page 108. SERVES 6

1 tablespoon butter
1/2 cup diced carrots
1/2 cup diced celery
1/2 teaspoon crab base*
1/2 teaspoon lobster base*
1/2 teaspoon shrimp base*
1 quart whipping cream
2 cups milk
1/4 cup sherry
1/8 teaspoon cumin, ground
1/8 teaspoon dill
3 cups cooked seafood
6 crêpe shells

* May substitute canned broth, bouillon or water.

Chef Deborah Van Plew

Seafood Quiche

1/2 cup butter
10 medium to large
  shrimp
1/2 pound scallops
3/4 cup crabmeat
1/4 teaspoon salt
1/8 teaspoon pepper
8 eggs
1 quart heavy cream
1 teaspoon thyme
2 cups grated Swiss
  cheese
2, 9" pie shells,
  unbaked

Heat a medium sauté pan and add the butter. Brown all of the seafood and season with half of the salt and pepper. Set aside.

In a separate bowl, whip the eggs lightly, then add the cream. Whip in the remaining salt, pepper and thyme. Fold the browned seafood and cheese into the egg mixture. Put half into each shell and bake at 325° for 45 minutes. Remove from the oven and let stand 15 minutes before serving.

YIELD: 8 LARGE SLICES

Chef Robert A. Fedorko,
Formerly of the Westin Resort

Seafood "Meatloaf" with Boursin Mushroom Gravy

Pureé flounder fillets in food processor with eggs and cream. Rough chop shrimp and blend by hand into flounder mixture with all other ingredients. Lightly grease a loaf pan and press mixture into pan. Cover loosely with foil and bake at 350 degrees for 30 minutes. Turn out loaf and serve in 1 inch thick slices with boursin mushroom gravy (recipe follows next page). SERVES 10

1 pound flounder fillets
3 eggs
1/2 cup heavy cream
1/2 pound raw shrimp, peeled and deveined
1 pound lump crabmeat
1/2 pound lobster meat
2 cups seasoned bread crumbs
2 tablespoons Old Bay seasoning
1 tablespoon chopped garlic
1/4 cup finely chopped parsley

Chef Richard Vaughan,
Spartina Grill

Boursin Mushroom Gravy

1/4 pound shiitake mushrooms, thinly sliced
1/4 pound oyster mushrooms, thinly sliced
1 tablespoon chopped garlic
1/2 cup melted butter
3/4 cup flour
2 teaspoons Grey Poupon mustard
1 quart heavy whipping cream
2, five ounce packages herbed boursin cheese

Sauté both mushrooms and garlic in butter for 5 minutes. Add flour and stir, forming a roux. Cook on low heat for 5 more minutes. Add mustard, cream and boursin and stir vigorously while cooking an additional 5 minutes. Remove from heat and serve with Seafood "Meatloaf."
SERVES 10

Chef Richard Vaughan,
Spartina Grill

Shrimp Pernod over Rice

Sauté the diced onion in 1 tablespoon of the butter and add the rice, chicken stock, salt and pepper. Simmer for 5 minutes. Cover and bake for 30 minutes in a 350° oven. Sauté the shrimp in 1 tablespoon of butter with the sliced onion and peppers until the vegetables start to soften. Add the basil, salt and pepper. Allow to cook for 3 minutes. Add the tomatoes and Pernod to taste. Allow Pernod to flame. Serve over rice.
SERVES 6

1/2 onion, diced
2 tablespoon butter
1 1/4 cups rice
2 cups chicken stock,*
   or chicken broth
salt and pepper
3 pounds large
   shrimp, cleaned and
   deveined
1 onion, sliced
1 red pepper, sliced
1 green pepper, sliced
pinch of basil
1 pint cherry tomatoes
2 - 4 tablespoons
   Pernod*

* See glossary.

Chef Mark Christian,
Aunt Chiladas

Shrimp Provencal

2 ounces olive oil
1 shallot, chopped
1 clove garlic, chopped
5 ounces fresh sliced
   mushrooms
1 pound shrimp 16/20
   count
8 ounces diced tomatoes
3 ounces lemon juice
3 1/2 ounces white
   wine
1 ounce fresh basil
   leaves
1 ounce fresh oregano
   leaves
1 ounce fresh thyme
   leaves
1 tablespoon Old Bay
   seasoning

Heat oil in large sauté pan to smoking point. Add chopped shallots and garlic, brown off. Add mushrooms, cooking them down slightly. Add shrimp to pan, cooking shrimp halfway done (slightly opaque.) Add tomatoes, lemon juice, white wine, fresh chopped herbs and Old Bay seasoning. Continue cooking until shrimp are done. Serve hot. Enjoy!

SERVES 2

Chef Paul Pinski,
Café at Belfair

Shrimp Scampi

Sauté the shrimp and garlic in the butter. When the shrimp is almost cooked, remove from the pan and add the sherry, chicken stock and lemon juice. Bring to a boil and reduce the heat. Blend in the bread crumbs. Add the parsley and shrimp. Simmer until the sauce thickens slightly. Serve with thinly sliced French bread and lemon wedges.
SERVES 2

10 large shrimp, peeled and deveined
1 tablespoon fresh garlic, minced
2 tablespoons clarified butter*
1/4 cup sherry
1/4 cup chicken stock,* or broth
1 tablespoon lemon juice
1/2 cup bread crumbs, finely chopped
1 tablespoon parsley, chopped

*See glossary.

Chef Jeff Hendrickson

189

Shrimp Zorba

2 tablespoons olive oil
5 large shrimp
1 splash Ouzo*
2 tomato slices, chopped very fine
1/2 teaspoon dill
salt and pepper to taste
1/2 teaspoon garlic
2-3 tablespoons heavy cream

* See glossary.

Sauté shrimp in oil till 1/4 - 1/2 way done. Flame with Ouzo. Add tomatoes, dill, salt, pepper and garlic. Cook one minute. Add heavy cream and cook on high heat until it thickens, stirring constantly. Serve over rice and with salad and pita.
SERVES 1

Chef Eric Foss,
Market Street Café

Smoked Caribbean Meat Pie

Heat the oil and add the onions, peppers, garlic, thyme, and parsley. Add the pork, olives, red peppers, tomatoes, and simmer until the liquid reduces and the mixture coats a spoon. Mix the sherry, vinegar and mustard until dissolved. Add to the meat and vegetables and mix well. Remove from the pan.

Combine the flour, salt and shortening. Rub the mixture together until it resembles coarse meal Pour ice water over the mixture and toss until the dough holds together. Roll the dough into a cylinder about 12" long and 2" in diameter. Cut into 2" segments, then roll each segment into a 6" circle. Put 1/3 cup of the warm filling mixture in the center of the circle and egg wash the edges. Fold the dough in half until the edges meet. With a floured fork, press the edges down to seal. Brush the surface of the pie with the melted butter and bake on a buttered sheet pan at 350 degrees for 20 minutes or until the crust is golden.
SERVES 6

Chef Sonny Tanksley

3 tablespoons olive oil
Finely chop:
  1 cup onion
  1/2 cup green pepper
  1 tablespoon garlic
  1 tablespoon fresh thyme
  1 tablespoon parsley
1, 2-pound smoked pork shoulder, minced
  2 tablespoons green and black olives
1 teaspoon red pepper, crushed
2 cups tomatoes, diced
2 tablespoons sherry
1 tablespoon balsamic vinegar
3/4 teaspoon dry mustard
2 1/2 cups flour
1/2 teaspoon salt
3/4 cup shortening
4-6 tablespoons ice water
1 egg, beaten
1/4 cup butter, melted

Smoked Chicken Breast with Apple Butter

2, 6-8 ounce chicken breasts
1 sweet apple, peeled, cored, diced and baked
4 tablespoons butter
1/2 teaspoon cinnamon
1/4 cup sugar

To prepare the apple butter, soften the butter to room temperature. Add the diced apple, cinnamon and sugar. Mix well.

To prepare the chicken, brush the chicken breasts with the apple butter. Smoke over hickory chips for two minutes on each side. Remove from the smoker and baste once again with the apple butter. Place the chicken in a 350° oven for 12-14 minutes or until done. Serve on a bed of lettuce or on a sandwich roll.

SERVES 2

Chef Robert A. Fedorko,
Formerly of the Westin Resort

Snapper Fillets with Orange, Tomato and Cilantro Sauce

Salt and pepper the fish. In a medium saucepan, simmer the orange juice, tomato, garlic, shallots, cilantro, white wine, salt and pepper. Reduce the heat and whisk in the butter 1 tablespoon at a time, allowing each to melt before adding the next one. Bake, poach, broil or charbroil the fish. Coat with the sauce.
SERVES 6

2 1/2 to 3 pounds
  snapper fillets
salt and pepper
2/3 cup orange juice
1 tomato, peeled,
  seeded, diced
1/2 teaspoon garlic,
  minced
2 tablespoons shallots,
  minced
1 tablespoon fresh
  cilantro
1/4 cup white wine
1 stick unsalted
  butter

Chef Dean A. Thomas,
Formerly of the Westin Resort

Steak, Wine-Growers Style

3 medium shallots,
peeled
1 medium onion
2 pieces anchovy fillets
2 pounds boneless
ribeye
salt and pepper
3 1/2 tablespoons
butter
1/2 cup red wine

Chop the shallots, onion and anchovy fillets into very small pieces, or purée in a blender. Set aside.

Salt and pepper the steak. Heat the butter in a frying pan until it foams. Add the steak and cook over moderate heat for 6 minutes each side for rare or 8 minutes each side for medium.

Remove the steak and set on a warm platter. Add the onion, shallots and anchovy mixture to the pan drippings. Cook until the onions are soft and begin to brown. Add the wine. Cook at a boil for 1-2 minutes until the sauce thickens to coat a spoon. Strain.

Serve the sauce over steak or in a gravy boat.
SERVES 4

Chef Dave Plemmons

Stuffed Chicken Legs with Mushrooms and Ham

8 cooked chicken legs
3 basil leaves
1 teaspoon butter
2 large shallots, diced
2 garlic cloves, diced
1/2 pound mushrooms, diced
6 tablespoons ham, diced
1 cup whipping cream
salt and pepper

Bone the chicken. Slice the basil leaves into very thin strips. In a saucepan, melt the butter. Add shallots, basil, garlic, mushrooms and ham. Cook for 10 minutes without browning, then add the cream and cook 10 minutes on medium heat. Add the salt and pepper. Stuff the chicken legs with the mixture, using string to hold everything together, roast in a 450° oven for 15 minutes. Remove the string and skewers and slice the chicken.
SERVES 8

Chef Jean-Loup Kunckler,
Formerly of The Gaslight

Stuffed Shells

1, 12-ounce package
jumbo pasta shells
2, 9-ounce frozen
creamed spinach (in
cook-in-pouch)
15-ounce package
ricotta cheese
1 cup mozzarella
cheese, shredded
1 teaspoon salt
1/4 teaspoon pepper
1/2 pound ground
beef*
1 quart marinara
sauce**

*May substitute
shrimp and scallops.

**May substitute a
cream seafood sauce.

Cook the shells as directed and drain. Prepare the spinach as directed on the pouch.

Open the spinach into a large bowl and cool slightly. Stir in the cheeses, salt and pepper. Stuff each shell with 1 tablespoon of mixture and place in an oven-proof pan. Cook the beef over medium heat until browned. Stir in the marinara sauce. Spoon the sauce over the shells. Cover with foil and bake at 350° for 30 minutes.

Note: this recipe will freeze well up to 3 months. Remove from freezer and bake for 50 minutes.

SERVES 10

Chef Deborah Van Plew

Tournedos au Poivre

Melt half of the butter in a large frying pan over medium-high heat. Add the steaks and sauté on both sides until medium rare. Remove from the pan. Set aside. Add the brandy, peppercorns, and shallots. Stir and ignite. When the flame dies down, add the brown gravy and red wine. Cook until sauce is reduced by 1/3. Stir in the remaining butter and parsley. Pour over steaks and serve. SERVES 4

8, 3-ounce tenderloin steaks
1 cup butter
1/2 cup brandy
2 teaspoons green peppercorns
2 teaspoons minced shallots
1 cup brown gravy
1/2 cup red wine
2 teaspoons parsley, chopped

Courtesy of Bev & Lou Gerber, Proprietors, Café Europa

Triggerfish with Sweet Pepper Pecan Confit

1 cup shelled pecans, chopped
3 tablespoons fresh oregano
1/2 cup bourbon
3 tablespoons lemon vinegar*
4, 6-ounce fillets of triggerfish
1/2 red bell pepper, chopped
1/2 yellow bell pepper, chopped
1 tablespoon sugar
4 tablespoons butter
1/4 cup white wine
salt
fresh cracked pepper

* White vinegar with the addition of a small amount of lemon.

Thoroughly mix the pecans, oregano, bourbon and vinegar. Pour over the fish and marinate for 48 hours.

Remove the fish and add the bell peppers and sugar to the pecan mixture and bake in a 350° oven until the liquid evaporates. Brush the fish with the butter and wine. Top with the pecan mixture. Salt and pepper to taste. Broil until brown.

SERVES 4

Chef Dean A. Thomas,
Formerly of The Westin Resort

198

Tuna Au Poivre with Lobster Sauce and Wilted Greens

4, 1" thick tuna steaks
salt and fresh cracked
* pepper*
butter
brandy for deglazing
* pan*

To prepare: At least two hours ahead of time; coat 1 side of quality 1" thick tuna steaks with salt and fresh cracked pepper. Combine in a large bowl, fresh greens, sliced onion and sliced shiitake mushrooms. In a heavy sauce pan, reduce by 1/2 the heavy cream and lobster base. Set aside to cool. Cook 1 1/4 pound lobster, cool, remove meat, cut into chunks and set aside.

When ready to serve: In a hot pan, add a pat of butter, sear the tuna fillets to medium rare turning once. Remove from heat and keep warm (not hot). Remove pan from heat. Deglaze with brandy (do not pour from bottle). Return pan to heat and burn off the brandy. Add the reduced cream and reduce to sauce consistency, season with salt and white pepper. Add lobster pieces and heat through. Right before serving, whisk in a dollop of softened butter.

Wilted Greens:
fresh, cleaned greens
* (your choice - I use*
* spinach)*
thin sliced red onion
thin sliced de-stemmed
* shiitake mushroom*
3-4 garlic cloves,
* smashed*
bacon or pancetta, cut
* into small pieces*

(continued on next page)

Lobster sauce:
1 quart heavy cream
1 teaspoon lobster
base *
salt & white pepper to
taste
1 1/4 pound lobster,
cooked, meat cut into
chunks

Garnish:
fresh chopped chives

* See glossary.

(continued from previous page)

In a separate pan: Render down good quality smoked bacon or pancetta, cut into small pieces. Add several cloves of smashed garlic. Cook 1 minute, taking care not to burn garlic. Add the greens mixture and toss well.

Transfer to plate: Mound of wilted greens, top with tuna steak and pour lobster sauce over and around the steak and greens. Garnish with chopped chives.

SERVES 4

Chef Brad Terhune,
Captain's Seafood

Veal Chops with Golden Almonds, Prosciutto, and Brandy Cream

3 tablespoons butter
1 cup sliced almonds
1 teaspoon garlic, chopped
1/4 cup prosciutto
1/4 cup brandy
1/2 cup demi-glace*
1/4 cup heavy cream
pinch of salt
pinch of pepper
1/4 cup oil
4, 1" thick veal chops

* See glossary.

To prepare the sauce, in a small pan melt the butter over medium heat. Add the almonds and garlic, being careful not to burn the garlic, and cook until brown. Add the prosciutto and cook for 3 minutes. Add the brandy, flame, then add demi-glace and cream. Simmer for 10 minutes. Salt and pepper to taste.

To prepare the veal, preheat the oven to 350°. Heat the oil in a pan and sear the chops on both sides. Place the chops in the oven and cook for 10 minutes. Place on a platter with the sauce and serve.

SERVES 4

Chef Richard Canestrari,
211 Park

Veal with Morel Mushrooms

1/2 cup dried morel
  mushrooms
1 shallot
8 slices veal top round,
  5 to 6-ounces each
salt and pepper
flour
1/4 cup cognac
16 ounces fresh heavy
  cream

Soak the mushrooms in water until soft, about 30 minutes. Cut in half and wash 4 to 5 times in water. Peel and chop the shallot very fine.

Salt and pepper each slice of the veal. Put flour on each side and pan-fry. Set aside. In same pan deglaze with the shallots, mushrooms, cognac and heavy cream. Bring to a boil and reduce until thick. Add the juices from the veal to the sauce and pour over the veal.

SERVES 8

Chef Claude Melchiorri,
Rendezvous Café

Viennese Wiener Schnitzel

Squeeze the juice from the lemon and set aside.

Put the flour mixture in a separate bowl and set aside.

Beat the eggs with 2 teaspoons salad oil in a separate bowl and set aside.

Chop, grind or crush the bread crumbs in a separate bowl. Set aside.

Pound out the veal with a mallet or the side of a heavy knife. Coat the veal with lemon and blot with a paper towel. Dredge the veal in seasoned flour, shaking off excess. Immerse the veal in the egg-oil mixture. Coat it with the bread crumbs and press the crumbs into the meat. Heat the remaining oil until very hot. Add the meat and reduce the heat to medium. Brown on both sides. SERVES 4

1 lemon
1 cup flour, seasoned
  with salt and pepper
2 eggs
1/4 cup salad oil
1 1/2 cups fresh bread
  crumbs
4, 4-ounce veal cutlets

Chef Dave Plemmons

Desserts

Almond Tuiles with Fresh Raspberries

Preheat the oven to 350°. Mix the sugar, flour, egg whites and salt. Beat to a thick batter. Add the almonds. Allow to sit 30 minutes.

Spray a cookie sheet with a nonstick spray, then pour about 4 1/2 teaspoons of batter per tuile. Bake 8-10 minutes until golden brown. Quickly place the hot tuiles over inverted cups to form baskets. Once cool, fill the baskets with the raspberries, sprinkled or tossed with powdered sugar.

To prepare the crème anglaise, scald the milk with the vanilla extract. Combine the sugar, cornstarch and egg yolks. Whisk until pale and creamy. Slowly add the milk. Place the mixture in a double boiler over hot water and whisk for 10 minutes until the sauce coats the back of a wooden spoon. Remove the bowl from the double boiler and rest it in ice water.

To serve, place a little sauce on each plate and place the tuile on the sauce. Garnish with a few raspberries and fresh sprigs of mint.
SERVES 4 - 6

Chef Jim McLain,
Callawassie Island

Tuiles:
3/4 cup powdered sugar, sifted
3/4 cup all-purpose flour
3 large egg whites
pinch of salt
2 tablespoons slivered almonds

Filling:
2 cups fresh raspberries
1/4 cup powdered sugar, sifted

Crème anglaise:
1 1/2 cups milk
2 teaspoons vanilla extract
1/2 cup sugar
1 teaspoon cornstarch
4 large egg yolks

Garnish:
1/2 cup fresh raspberries
2 stems fresh mint

Crust (Pre-bake):
8 tablespoons unsalted
 butter (softened)
1 1/3 cup pastry flour or
 1 1/2 cup all-purpose
1/8 teaspoon salt
1/8 teaspoon baking
 powder
3 ounces cream cheese
1 1/2 tablespoons ice
 water
1 1/2 teaspoons cider
 vinegar

Cheesecake Tart:
1 1/2 pounds poached
 apricots or canned
 apricots in syrup
1 cup apricot preserves
2 teaspoons Grand
 Marnier
3 1/2 tablespoons cream
 cheese
pinch of cinnamon
pinch of nutmeg
3/4 cup heavy cream
1 egg + 1 yolk
2 tablespoons egg white

Apricot Cheesecake Tart

For pie crust: Mix all ingredients well and form a shell in a pie pan. Pre-bake.

Drain apricots well, cut side down. Heat the preserves, then stir in 1 teaspoon Grand Marnier. Brush mixture on the bottom of crust (don't use it all). In a food processor, add cream cheese, cinnamon and nutmeg, blend until smooth. Add heavy cream, yolk and whites along with remaining Grand Marnier. (The mixture will be lumpy.) Pour half the mixture into pre-baked pie shell. Place the apricots on (rounded side up). Carefully poor remaining filling on top (around apricots so it doesn't coat the tops). Bake 30-35 minutes at 375°. Brush on remaining glaze.
SERVES 8-10

Chef Amanda Phillips,
Hyatt Regency

Biscotti

Cream together the butter and sugar. Add flour, baking powder and eggs. Add nuts. Form into 2 logs on a cookie sheet. Bake until brown. Remove from the oven and cut into 1/2 inch slices. Bake again until the slices are golden brown and crispy.

YEILD: ABOUT 20 BISCOTTI

4 ounces butter
1 1/2 cups sugar
4 cups flour
2 teaspoons baking
  powder
4 eggs
1 1/2 cups toasted
  almonds
3/4 cups toasted
  pistachios

Pastry Chef Jennifer Webb,
Westin Resort

Layered "Martini" with Chocolate Baileys and Grand Marnier White Chocolate Mousse

For Chocolate Baileys Mousse:

10 ounces semi sweet chocolate

2 eggs

2 egg yolks

5 tablespoons Baileys Irish Cream liqueur

2 tablespoons sugar

20 ounces stiff whipped cream

For Grand Marnier White Chocolate Mousse:

10 ounces white chocolate

2 eggs

2 egg yolks

3 tablespoons Grand Marnier liqueur

2 tablespoons sugar

15 ounces stiff whipped cream

Chocolate Baileys Mousse: In a stainless steel bowl, melt chocolate over double boiler until smooth, being careful not to scorch. Remove from heat. In separate stainless steel bowl, whisk together eggs, sugar and liqueur over double boiler until doubled in volume and thick (about 8 to 10 minutes.) Combine melted chocolate into egg mixture, cool a bit. Fold into whipped cream and refrigerate for at least 1 hour.

Grand Marnier White Chocolate Mousse: In a stainless steel bowl, melt white chocolate over double boiler until smooth. Remove from heat. In separate stainless steel bowl, whisk eggs, sugar and liqueur over double boiler until doubled in volume and thick (about 8 to 10 minutes). Combine melted chocolate into egg mixture, cool. Fold into

(continued on next page)

210

(continued from previous page)
whip cream and refrigerate for at least 1 hour.

Nut Brittle: Combine butter and sugar with wooden spoon, add heavy cream and cool. Stir in chopped almonds and flour. Spread on non stick baking pan and bake at 375° (for 10-15 minutes or until golden brown. Remove from oven and cool for at least 1 hour. Break up the brittle, reserving larger pieces for garnish and smaller pieces for the layering process (see assembly, below).

Assembly: Sprinkle small amount of nut brittle in the bottom of 4 martini glasses. Layer Baileys chocolate mousse 1/3 of the way up the glass, sprinkle more nut brittle over that, layer Grand Marnier white chocolate mousse on top of that. Repeat alternate layers of each mousse to the top of the glass. Be sure to sprinkle the nut brittle in-between each layer! With a hot, butter knife smooth top layer of mousse even with glass. Garnish with larger pieces of nut brittle.

YIELD: 4

For Nut Brittle:
8 ounces butter, melted
1 cup sugar
4 tablespoons heavy cream
3 cups chopped almonds
2 tablespoons flour

Chef De Cuisine Eric Sayers,
CQ's Restaurant

Chocolate Chip Pie

2 medium eggs
1/2 cup sugar
1/2 cup brown sugar
1/4 cup flour
1 cup melted butter,
    cooled
3/4 cup semisweet
    chocolate chips
1/2 cup walnuts,
    chopped
1, 9" pie shell,
    uncooked

Beat the eggs in a bowl, adding the sugar, brown sugar and flour. Continuing to mix, add the butter, then the chocolate chips and walnuts. Mix well. Pour into the pie shell and bake at 325° until browned.

Note: Bake the pie immediately. Do not let it stand after it is mixed.

SERVES 8

Chef Anthony Mastropole,
Formerly of The Hyatt Regency

Chocolate Mousse Pie

To prepare the crust, combine the crumbs and the butter. Press onto the bottom and sides of a 10" springform pan. Chill for 30 minutes.

For filling: soften the chocolate in a double boiler or microwave. Scrape into a bowl and add 2 whole eggs. Mix well, keeping the mixture warm. Add the 4 egg yolks and mix until blended.

Whip the cream with powdered sugar until soft peaks form. Set aside.

Beat the egg whites until stiff but not dry. Stir a little of the cream mixture and a little of the egg whites into the chocolate mixture to lighten. Fold in the remaining cream and the remaining egg whites until completely blended. Pour into the crust and chill for 6 hours. After the pie has set, whip the remaining cups of heavy cream, powdered sugar and vanilla. Loosen the crust of the pie on all sides, using a sharp knife. Remove from the springform pan. Spread the whipped cream over the top of the mousse. Sprinkle the top with shaved chocolate and serve.

SERVES 14

Chef Anthony Mastropole,
Formerly of the Hyatt Regency

Crust:
3 cups Oreo cookie crumbs
1/2 cup unsalted butter, melted

Filling:
2 cups semi-sweet chocolate
2 medium eggs
4 medium eggs, separated
2 cups heavy cream
6 tablespoons powdered sugar

Topping:
2 cups heavy cream
1/4 cup powdered sugar
1 teaspoon vanilla
semi-sweet chocolate, shaved

Chocolate Tia Maria Soufflé

2/3 cup semi-
sweet chocolate
3 tablespoons water
4 egg yolks
10 tablespoons
granulated sugar
2 tablespoons Tia
Maria
1/2 teaspoon
cinnamon, ground
6 egg whites
1 pinch salt
1 tablespoon butter,
melted
powdered sugar

Preheat the oven to 425°. Melt the chocolate with the water in a microwave on medium for 3-4 minutes.

In a bowl, beat the egg yolks and 6 table-spoons of sugar until pale and creamy. Stir in the chocolate. Add the Tia Maria and the cinnamon and set aside.

In a bowl, beat the egg whites and the salt until stiff peaks form. Fold half of the egg whites into the chocolate mixture until the color is uni-form. Lightly fold in the rest of the egg whites. Uniformity of color is not necessary at this stage.

Butter 4 small soufflé dishes, coating the inside with the remaining 4 tablespoons of sugar. Pour the batter into each and smooth. Bake for 10-20 minutes until the soufflés are twice their origi-nal height. Remove from the oven and sprinkle with the powdered sugar, serving immediately.
SERVES 4

*Chef Jim McLain,
Callawassie Island*

214

Double Chocolate Torte with White Chocolate Sauce

Blend the first four pastry ingredients until it resembles coarse meal. Add the water and toss until the water is absorbed. Form a ball and knead lightly to distribute the fat. Dust with flour and chill for 30 minutes. Grease a tart pan with a non-stick spray. Roll the dough on a floured surface until wider than the pan. Line the pan with dough and pre-bake for 15 minutes.

Blend the chocolate and the butter until smooth. Combine the eggs and the salt. Whisk until foamy. Gradually add the sugar and vanilla and whip until a ribbon forms when you remove the whisk. Add the chocolate mixture and the flour. Blend well. Pour into the shell and bake at 375° for 25-30 minutes.

To prepare the sauce, melt the white chocolate in a double boiler for about 8 - 10 minutes. Transfer it to a bowl and cool slightly. Add the sugar and whisk until smooth. Mix in the cream, butter and salt. To serve, slice the torte and cover with the white chocolate sauce. SERVES 6 - 8

Chef Jim McLain,
Callawassie Island

Pastry:
1 1/4 cups all-purpose flour
3/4 stick unsalted butter
2 tablespoons vegetable shortening
1/4 teaspoon salt
3 tablespoons ice water

Chocolate Filling:
1 cup semi-sweet chocolate
1/2 cup unsalted butter
4 eggs
1/4 teaspoon salt
2 cups sugar
1 1/2 teaspoons vanilla
1 cup all-purpose flour, sifted

White Chocolate Sauce:
1 1/2 cups white chocolate
3 cups powdered sugar, sifted
3/4 cup heavy cream
3 tablespoons unsalted butter, softened
2 pinches of salt

215

Eggnog Custard

2 1/2 cups
 half-and-half
1 vanilla bean
8 large egg yolks
1/3 cup sugar
3 tablespoons bourbon
1/8 teaspoon nutmeg

Combine all ingredients and blend well with a whisk. Spray 8 ceramic oven proof baking dishes with Pam. Ladle the mixture into each cup. Bake in a 350° oven in a water bath for approximately 1 hour.

Serving suggestion: Turn the custard out onto a plate and serve with gingerbread wafers. See page 220 for recipe.

SERVES 8

Pastry Chef Jennifer Webb,
Westin Resort

Gascon Apple Pie

Gently toss the apples with the sugars, salt and Armagnac or Cognac. Cover and allow to sit at room temperature for 2 hours and up to overnight. Drain the apples reserving the juice. Reduce the juice to about 3 tablespoons; let cool, then add orange flower water. Add the juice mixture to the apples along with the walnuts. Brush bottom of the pie pan with melted butter. Take phyllo dough and line the pan with 7 sheets, buttering each one and allowing some to drape over the pan. Bring the over hanging phyllo up and over the apples. Butter 2 sheets of phyllo, fold in half crosswise and place on top of apples. Tuck ends into side of the pan. There will be a depression in the center. Butter another sheet of phyllo and cut in half. Gather up each loose piece and ruffle and arrange it toward the center of the pie to fill the depression. Butter the final piece of phyllo and fold it long ways into thirds. Coil it loosely to form a rose and place in the center. Bake at 375° for 50 to 60 minutes until phyllo is golden brown.
SERVES 8-10

Chef Amanda Phillips,
Hyatt Regency

1 2/3 pounds apples (peeled, cored and sliced)
3 tablespoons sugar
3 tablespoons brown sugar
1/8 teaspoon salt
1/3 cup Armagnac* or Cognac
1 1/2 tablespoons orange flower water**
3/4 cup walnuts (lightly toasted)
7 tablespoons melted butter
12 sheets phyllo dough
powdered sugar (optional)

* A French brandy from Gascony.
** Orange flower water: 1/2 teaspoon citrus oil & 1 tablespoon grated zest of orange

2 peaches, peeled, pitted, and coarsely chopped

1 cup sugar

2 tablespoons quick cooking tapioca

1 tablespoon lemon juice

2 cups heavy cream

1/2 cup half and half

10 large egg yolks

1/2 cup sugar

1 tablespoon vanilla extract

2 tablespoons ginger purée

4 tablespoons brown sugar

Ginger Peach Creme Brûlée

To prepare the ginger purée: In a medium saucepan, combine all of the ingredients. Bring to a simmer over medium high heat and cook until tender, about 45 minutes, stirring often. Transfer to a food processor and purée until smooth. Strain. Reserve in the refrigerator for up to 1 month or freeze.

Preheat the oven to 350°. In a medium bowl, combine the peaches, sugar, tapioca and lemon juice. Mix until well combined and allow to set for 15 minutes. Pour into an ovenproof glass dish and bake until brown and bubbly, about 30 minutes. Remove from the oven and allow to cool. In a medium size saucepan, scald the cream and half and half over medium high heat. Remove from the heat.

In a medium bowl, combine the egg yolks, sugar and vanilla, beat with a wire whisk until light. Slowly add the hot cream and ginger purée, whisking until smooth. Strain through a fine sieve.

(continued on next page)

218

(continued from previous page)

Divide the peach mixture among 4 custard dishes. Top with the custard to 1/4" below the top edge. Place the custards in a hot water bath in the lower third of the oven. Cook until the custard is set and lightly tanned on top, about 20 - 25 minutes. Remove to a cake rack and allow to cool. Cover and refrigerate for 6 - 8 hours before serving.

To serve, preheat the broiler. Evenly spread the brown sugar across the tops of the custard. Place the custards under the broiler, allowing the tops to caramelize but not burn. (Propane blow torches also work very well.) Allow to cool for several minutes before serving.

SERVES 4

Ginger Purée:
2 cups peeled and
   minced ginger
1/2 cup fresh lemon
   juice
1/2 cup sugar
1/4 cup water

Chef Keith Josefiak,
Starfire

Gingerbread Wafers

1 cup butter
1 1/2 cups brown
   sugar
1 cup molasses
2 cups flour
1/4 teaspoon baking
   soda
1/4 teaspoon
   cinnamon
1/4 teaspoon ginger
1 teaspoon salt
1/4 teaspoon ground
   cloves
2 cups cold water
   (added to mixture,
   if necessary to keep
   moist)

Cream butter and brown sugar. Add molasses to blend. Add dry ingredients. Roll out and cut into any shape desired. Bake at 350° for approximately 15-20 minutes.

YIELD: 20 - 25 WAFERS

Pastry Chef Jennifer Webb,
Westin Resort

220

Keylime Pie

Make crust by combining saltines, sugar and melted butter. Mix yolks, keylime, lime rind and condensed milk. Form crust in 9" pie pan and add keylime mixture. Bake 12 minutes at 300°. Cool before serving.
SERVES 8-10

Crust:
2 cups saltine cracker
crumbs
1/2 cup sugar
1/2 cup melted butter

Filling:
6 yolks
1 cup squeezed
keylime juice
1 tablespoon grated
lime rind
28 ounces sweetened
condensed milk

Chef John Briody,
Colleton River Plantation

Macadamia Nut Pie

10 eggs
1 3/4 cups light brown
  sugar
1 1/4 cups light corn
  syrup
1 teaspoon salt
1/4 cup dark rum
1/4 pound butter,
  melted
1 pie dough for a 10"
  deep-dish pie
4 cups whole maca-
  damia nuts, roasted

Beat the eggs until light colored (do not over-beat). Add the sugar, corn syrup, salt and rum. Stir until the sugar is dissolved. Stir in the melted butter. Roll out your pie dough into a 10" pan. Place the nuts into the pie shell. Pour the mixture over the nuts in the pie shell. Bake at 325° for about 1 3/4 hours.

YIELD: 1 PIE

Chef Steve Hancotte,
Stripes

Milk Chocolate Creme Caramel

For caramel:
2 cups sugar
1 cup water

In a small saucepan, stir sugar and water together over medium-high heat, boil until the sugar turns medium-brown, or about the color of a new penny.) Pour this caramel in a thin layer into the bottom of five or six, 6-ounce individual baking dishes. These dishes should be warmed, or the caramel may shatter them.

1 quart half-and-half
3/4 cup + 1 tablespoon
sugar
1 vanilla bean
1 cinnamon stick
7 egg yolks
3 whole eggs
7 ounces milk chocolate

Place the half and half, sugar, vanilla bean and cinnamon stick in a 2-quart saucepan. Bring to a boil. While this is heating, whisk egg yolks and whole eggs together in a separate bowl. When the half and half begins to boil, remove it from heat. Stir in the milk chocolate until it melts. Pour 1/3 of the half-and-half into the eggs, and stir. Pour back into the remaining liquid, and stir. Pour mixture into the prepared baking dishes. Bake at 325°, in a water bath, until set, approximately 1 hour. Remove from oven, and let cool to room temperature. Chill before unmolding.
SERVES 6

Pastry Chef Owen Smith,
Café Europa

Peanut Butter Pie with Fudge Topping

Crust:
1 cup graham cracker crumbs
1/4 cup sugar
1/2 stick butter, melted

Filling:
8 ounces cream cheese, softened
1 cup chunky peanut butter
1 cup + 2 tablespoons powdered sugar
2 tablespoons butter
1/2 cup chilled whipping cream
1 tablespoon vanilla extract

Topping:
1/2 cup whipping cream
3/4 cup semi-sweet chocolate chips

To prepare the crust, butter a 9" pie pan. Mix all of the ingredients. Press into the pan and chill for 30 minutes.

To prepare the filling, beat the cream cheese and peanut butter, using an electric mixer. Add 1 cup of the powdered sugar and the butter. Beat until fluffy. In a separate bowl whip the cream until soft peaks form. Add the remaining 2 tablespoons powdered sugar and the vanilla and whip until stiff. Fold 1/4 of this into the peanut butter mixture. Fold in the remaining cream. Spoon the filling into the crust and chill a minimum of 3 hours.

To prepare the topping, bring the cream to a boil in a heavy saucepan. Add the chocolate and stir until smooth. Cool to lukewarm. Spread on the pie and chill for 2 more hours.

SERVES 8

Chef Richard Canestrari,
211 Park

224

Pears in Red Wine

Peel, core and cut the pears in half. Place the pears in a pan just large enough to hold them. Add the remaining ingredients and cover. Bring to a boil. Reduce to a slow simmer for 30 minutes.

Lift the pears out and place in a bowl. Spoon the sauce over them. Baste occasionally.

Refrigerate overnight. Spoon the sauce over the pears again before serving.

SERVES 4

4 medium smooth-skinned pears*
juice of 1 lemon
1/2 cup sugar
1 cup red wine
1 vanilla bean, split lengthwise
1 sprig fresh thyme
2 peppercorns
1 clove
4 tablespoons crème de cassis**

*May substitute 8 very small pears, unpeeled.

** See glossary.

Chef Dave Plemmons

225

Potato Chip Cookies

2 pounds butter
1 pound sugar
2 pounds crushed
  potato chips
2 pounds flour

Cream butter and sugar. Blend in potato chips. Mix flour into mixture until well blended. Bake at 350°for 10 minutes or until golden brown.
YIELD: 6 DOZEN

Chef Ann M. Mitchell,
Hyatt Regency

226

Sour Cream Cheesecake

20 *ounces cream cheese*

1 *cup granulated sugar*

2 *teaspoons lemon juice*

1 *teaspoon vanilla*
 extract

3 *eggs*

16 *ounces sour cream*

Grease and flour the sides of 1, 9-inch springform pan, and preheat the oven to 350°.

In a mixing bowl, cream the cream cheese and sugar until it is light and fluffy and there are no lumps left. Add the lemon juice and vanilla extract, and blend well. Scrape the sides of the mixing bowl, and cream for a few more seconds. Add the eggs, one at a time, blending well— after each addition, scrape the sides of the mixing bowl and cream a few more seconds. Blend in the sour cream.

Place a small pan of water on the floor or bottom rack of the oven. This will keep the oven moist during baking Pour the batter into a springform pan, and bake for 46 minutes. After 46 minutes, turn the oven off, and let the cake cool in the oven for another 45 minutes before removing it. Cool the cake to room temperature, then refrigerate overnight before serving it.

Note: This is a self-crusting cheesecake, so it is not essential to add any crust before baking. However, if you do choose to, graham cracker crumbs, crushed Oreos, or crushed gingersnaps work well. Line the bottom of the pan with the crumbs, and bake for 8 to 10 minutes at 350° before baking the cheesecake.

YIELD: 1 CAKE

Pastry Chef Owen Smith,
Café Europa

Tiramisu

1 chocolate sponge
cake, 10" round x
1 1/2" thick
2 1/4, 8-ounce
packages cream
cheese
1 1/2 cups powdered
sugar
3 cups heavy cream
3 tablespoons, plus 1/3
cup Kahlua
1/2 teaspoon espresso
1 teaspoon vanilla

Sprinkle the sponge cake with 3 tablespoons of Kahlua. In a large bowl, whip the cream cheese until smooth. Mix in the powdered sugar. Slowly add the cream and beat until thickened. Add the rest of the Kahlua, the espresso and vanilla to the mixture. Beat until thick - approximately 1 minute. Spread the cream cheese mixture on top of the cake and dust with the cocoa powder, leaving the sides bare. Refrigerate for at least 2 hours.

YIELD: 1 CAKE

*Chef Anthony Mastropole,
formerly of the Hyatt Regency*

Tropical Cheesecake

To prepare the crust, grease an 8" springform pan. Melt the butter in a small pan on low heat. Stir in the crushed Oreo cookies. Press into the greased pan. Set aside.

To prepare the filling, beat the cream cheese, sour cream, yogurt, 1/4 cup plus 2 tablespoons of sugar and the egg yolks until smooth. Combine the gelatin and the water in a small pan. Simmer to dissove the gelatin. Stir into the cheese mixture. Fold the whipped cream into the cheese mixture. Beat the egg whites with the remaining sugar until soft peaks form and fold into the cheese mixture. Spoon the filling into the prepared crust. Chill 2 to 3 hours until set.

Arrange cut fruit on the cheese cake. Brush with 1/4 cup melted apricot jelly.
SERVES 8 - 10

1/3 cup sweet butter
1 3/4 cups Oreo
cookies, crushed
1 1/2, 8-ounce
packages cream
cheese, softened
2/3 cup sour cream
2/3 cup plain yogurt
1/2 cup sugar
3 eggs, separated
1 tablespoon plus 1
teaspoon unflavored
gelatin
2 tablespoons water
2/3 cup whipping
cream, whipped
2 cups assorted fresh
fruit
apricot jelly

Chef Ed Buffkin

Simple syrup:
1 pound sugar
4 ounces water

Tropical Orange Soufflé

Soufflé:
8 egg yolks
1 cup orange juice
3 cups heavy cream
10 oranges

Cook sugar and water to 240°. Whip the yolks until light and foamy. Add simple syrup to yolks slowly. Add orange juice slowly. Cool down. Whip the heavy cream. Fold cream into orange mixture. Place mixture into orange molds and freeze.

For orange molds, slice oranges in half, squeeze juice out, be careful not to tear. Scrape centers out then fill with soufflé mixture.
YIELD: 20, 3-OUNCE ORANGE HALVES

Chef Amanda Phillips,
Hyatt Regency

Vanilla Bean Créme Brûlée

Preheat oven to 325°. Slice the vanilla bean in half lengthwise, and scrape the contents into a 2-quart saucepan. Add the sliced vanilla bean, the heavy cream and both the sugars. Bring to a simmer over medium heat on the stove.

While the cream is heating, stir the yolks and the whole eggs together in a separate bowl. When the cream begins to steam, remove from the heat and stir half of the cream into the eggs. Stir the egg mixture back into the remaining cream, and strain the mixture into a bowl.

Pour the cream into seven 6-ounce baking dishes. Place these dishes in a larger casserole dish, then fill it with water to just below the top of the baking cups. Bake for approximately 1 hour and 15 minutes, or until the custard is set. Remove from the oven, and cool before serving.
SERVES 7

Pastry Chef Owen Smith,
Café Europa

1 vanilla bean
1 quart heavy cream
3/4 cup granulated sugar
1 tablespoon brown sugar
7 egg yolks
2 whole eggs

Glossary

AL DENTE
Describes pasta or vegetables lightly cooked, offering a slight resistance when bitten into, yet not soft or overcooked.

ALL SPICE
A sweet flavored combination of cloves, cinnamon and nutmeg.

ASIAGO
A semi-firm Italian cheese with a rich, nutty flavor.

BASES
All bases used in this book are Minor's products and can be found in most grocery stores. They come in a variety of seafood flavors, which include clam, crab, lobster and shrimp. Call 1-800-827-8328.

BEARNAISE SAUCE
Hollandaise sauce with the addition of tarragon.

BECHAMEL SAUCE
Basic French white sauce made by stirring milk into a butter-flour roux. Named after its innventor, Louis XIV's steward, Louis de Béchamel.

BLUE POINT MUSSELLS
The most common, abundant mussel, found along the Mediterranean, Atlantic and Pacific coasts.

BOURSIN
White, smooth cheese with a buttery texture.

BOUQUET GARNI
Herbs tied together or wrapped in cheesecloth (parsley, thyme and a bayleaf) used to flavor soups, stews and broths.

BRUNOISE
A mixture of vegetables that have been fine diced.

CANNELLINI
Large, white Italian bean.

CARPACCIO
An Italian dish consisting of thin shavings of raw beef, or fish.

CHAMBORD
A raspberry flavored liqueur.

CHANTERELLE
A wild mushroom with a nutty, sometimes fruity flavor. Can be found dried or canned in many suppermarkets. Known to grow in the Pacific Northwest and East Coast, but mostly imported from Europe.

CHERVIL
A member of the parsley family with a mild flavor. Also called cicily and sweet cicily.

CHEVRE CHEESE
A pure white, goatsmilk cheese with a tart flavor. Chèvre is French for "goat." Included are Bucheron and Montrachet. "Pur Chèvre" ensures that the cheese is made entirely from goat's milk; if this designation is not on the label, it may have the addition of cows milk.

CHICKEN STOCK
A strained liquid that is the result of cooking chicken and seasonings in water. Canned broth, bouillon or water may be substituted.

CHIFFONADE
Thin strips or shreds of vegetables.

CLAM BASE
See under BASES.

CLARIFIED BUTTER
Unsalted butter very slowly melted. This allows the milk solids to separate and sink to the bottom. What is left is clear or "clarified" butter with a higher smoking point which can be used to cook at higher temperatures.

COBIA
A white meat fish that is flaky, not oily and moderate in flavor. For information on this or any other fish or shellfish, call the US Government Hotline at 1-800-332-4010.

CONFIT
Ancient meat preserving method, usually duck, goose or pork, salted and slowly cooked in its own fat. The meat is then placed in a crock or pot and covered with its cooking fat which acts as a seal and preservative.

COULIS
A thick purée or sauce.

COURT BOUILLON
A broth made by cooking various herbs and vegetables in water for about 30 minutes. These usually include an onion studded with cloves, celery, carrots and a bouquet garni.

CORNICHON
French for "gherkin," corinchons are crisp, tart pickles made from tiny gherkin cucumbers.

CRAB BASE
See under BASES.

CREME DE CASSIS
Black currant-flavored liqueur.

DEGLAZE
This is done by heating a small amount of liquid (usually wine or stock) in the bottom of a pan after the food and excess fat have been removed, to loosen the browned bits of food which becomes the base for a sauce to be used on the foot prepared in the pan.

DEMI-GLACE
A combination of beef stock, madeira or sherry and tomato paste, reduced by half. A nice brown gravy will also work well in a pinch.

DAIKON
From the Japanese words dai (large) and kon (root) this vegetable is in fact a large asian radish with a sweet, fresh flavor.

FISH HOTLINE
For more information, call 1-800-332-4010.

FISH STOCK
Stock is strained liquid that is the result of cooking vegetables, meat, or fish bones and other seasoning ingredients in water.

FLAMBE
French for "flamed" or "flaming", refers to pouring of small amount of liquor over certain foods and igniting just before serving.

FLUTED
A grooved pattern in certain fruits and vegetables strictly for show.

GLACAGE
A glaze or glossy coating.

JERK SPICE
Dry seasoning blend. Usually a combo of chiles, thyme, spices (such as cinnmon, ginger and clove or allspice) garlic and onions. Used primarily in preparation of grilled meat.

JICAMA
Sometimes referred to as the Mexican potato, jicama has a water chestnut-like texture and a sweet, nutty flavor. Good both raw and cooked.

JULIENNE
Thin, matchstick cuts of food such as carrots or potatoes. Often used as a garnish.

LOBSTER BASE
See under BASES.

MORNAY SAUCE
A béchamel sauce to which cheese has been added. Usually Parmesan or Swiss.

NEUFCHATEL CHEESE
The French, orginal version of American cream cheese.

OLD BAY® SEASONING
A seafood spice, made by McCormick spices, available in most grocery stores. Call 1-800-632-5847 for more information.

OUZO
A clear, sweet, anise-flavored liqueur from Greece.

PANCETTA
Italian bacon cured with salt and spices but not smoked. Salty, flavorful.

PASILLA CHILE
Rich flavored, medium hot, blackish brown in color, also called chile negro. Sold whole or powdered.

PAPILLOTE
The French term for paper frills used to decorate tips of rib bones, such as those on Crown Roasts. 'En Papillote' refers to flood baked inside of greased parchment paper.

PERNOD
A licorice-flavored liqueur similar to absinthe.

RADICCHIO
A red-leafed Italian chicory ofter used as a salad green. The most common varieties used in the U.S. are Verona and Treviso.

RED SWISS CHARD
Also called ruby chard, a member of the beet family grown for its tender greens and crisp stalks.

ROSETTES
Decorative shape such as a flower, star, etc.

ROTELLE
Small, round pasta which resembles a wheel with spokes.

ROUX
A mixture, usually equal parts of flour and butter, cooked slowly over a low heat, used to thicken sauces, gravies and soups or stews.

SEASON ALL
Regular salt combined with other flavoring ingredients.

SHIITAKE
Also called golden oak, this dark-brown mushroom has a delicious, full-bodied flavor. The average size of the cap is 3 to 6 inches.

SHRIMP BASE
See under BASES.

STILTON
One of the finest English blue cheeses. Made from whole cow's milk.

SWEAT
Ingredients cooked in a small abount of fat over a low heat, covered. This ensures softening without browning, and cooking in natural juices.

TAHINI
A thick paste made of ground sesame seed.

TASSO HAM
Lean chunk of cured pork seasoned with garlic, red pepper, filé powder and other herbs and spices.

TERRINE
A container used for cooking patés.

USDA MEAT & POULTRY HOTLINE
For more information, call 1-800-535-4555.

WAHOO
Similar to Albacore, the Wahoo is a slightly sweet, fine, white fish. Usually baked, broiled or grilled.

WATER BATH
The process of cooking food by placing it in a container in a large, shallow pan of warm water which surrounds the food with gentle heat.

Index

242

244

245

ORDER FORMS

Use the order forms below for obtaining additional copies of this cookbook.

MAIL TO:

THE CHEFS OF HILTON HEAD
Southern Islands Publishing
PO Box 69
Beaufort, SC 29901

Please send me _____ copies of The Chefs of Hilton Head at $13.95, plus $1.75 postage and handling, per book. S.C. residents add 5% sales tax.

Enclosed is my check or money order for $_____.

Name _____

Address _____

City, State, Zip _____

Please send me _____ copies of The Chefs of Hilton Head at $13.95, plus $1.75 postage and handling, per book. S.C. residents add 5% sales tax.

Enclosed is my check or money order for $_____.

Name _____

Address _____

City, State, Zip _____